FROM THE MINUTE
YOU DECIDE ON YOUR DESTINATION
TO THE SECOND
YOUR FOOT TOUCHES THE GROUND.

SUPERFLIER

SHOWS YOU THE WAY TO

CHOOSE A TRAVEL AGENT

APPLY FOR A PASSPORT

FIND THE BEST FARE

GET YOUR TICKET

PACK YOUR BAGS

FIND YOUR WAY AROUND
THE MAJOR AIRPORTS

GET THE BEST SEAT
(AHEAD OF TIME) AND

ENJOY YOUR FLIGHT

AND TELLS YOU

WHAT TO DO IF
SOMETHING GOES WRONG

WHO'S PAYING ATTENTION
TO YOUR COMPLAINTS

AND GIVES

INNUMERABLE TRAVEL TIPS

HAVE NO FEAR!

IS HERE!

THE AIR TRAVELER'S HANDBOOK

SUPER FLIER

THE ASSERTIVE PASSENGER'S GUIDE

BY LAURA TORBET AND KALIA LULOW

TABLE OF CONTENTS

ACKNOWLEDGMENTS

We would like to thank all the people who shared their time and information with us so that we could compile this volume. Far more people fall into this category than we can possibly mention by name but we would like to mention a special few.

Without the two travel agents who offered us guidance and advice, this book would not have gotten off the ground. They are two of the most savvy travel agents around, and you'd be lucky to have them working for you.

Viola's Travel Service, Inc.
Viola Rubenstone, President
117 South 9th Street
Philadelphia, Pennsylvania 19107

Paramount Travel Service
Shirlee A. Rousseau, President
225 Park Avenue South
New York, New York 10003

Our thanks to the following folks, too: Hap Hatton; Kathy Saluk, American Airlines, New York; Larry Nobel, Aviation Consumer Action Project; Mr. Paul Reneau, Air Line Pilots Association; Office of the Consumer Advocate; Civil Aeronautics Board; Airline Passengers Association; National Transportation Safety Board; Federal Aviation

Administration; Flight Safety Foundation; American Society of Travel Agents; International Civil Aviation Organization; Air Transport Association of America; International Air Transport Association; and all the airport, airline and aircraft companies that supplied us with information on their operations.

INTRODUCTION

SUPERFLIER: THE AIR TRAVELER'S HANDBOOK, is a consumer guide to the *ins* and *outs* of air travel. It explores everything from the mysteries of today's air fares to the hidden corridors of the world's major international airports. Whether you are making your first flight or your 1000th, this book contains information that will make air traveling more efficient and more pleasurable for you.

SUPERFLIER takes the hesitant or novice air traveler through the steps involved in flying: selecting a travel agent, applying for a passport, ticketing, baggage regulations, negotiating the airport maze, seat selection, checking in, the security check, inflight procedures, customs and immigration, plus traveler's tips.

SUPERFLIER explores the *rights* of air travel consumers and the *wrongs* that are done them. And then it takes a look at who's running the show—the organizations in government and private industry that regulate the airlines; who's on your side—which organizations are defending your rights; and who to complain to to make sure your rights are not violated. Included is information on overbooking, delayed departures and lost or damaged baggage.

SUPERFLIER takes a detailed look at all major U.S. scheduled airlines, many international companies and the best-known supplementals—their routes, their services, their records—and lets you know what consumer surveys have revealed the best and worst travel experiences to be.

SUPERFLIER reveals the meaning behind the air fare lingo. What air fares are available? What do the fares mean to you? What are the savings and advantages to all the different fare plans?

SUPERFLIER takes you to ten major airports in the U.S. and six abroad. Descriptions of the services, facilities and layouts of all the airports help you find your way around these awesome complexes. In addition, there is a report on the worst airports in the world.

SUPERFLIER gives you detailed information about airline seat selection, airlines' headquarter addresses and phone numbers, travelers' tips and more—in a chock-full appendix.

**SUPERFLIER MAKES YOU A TRAVEL PRO!
WELCOME ABOARD!**

CHAPTER ONE
EASY RIDER

Over 200 million passengers cruise the airways of America every year. What this vast group of people all have in common is the desire for a safe and comfortable flight, free of confusion and inconvenience. If you are part of this ever-expanding group of travelers or if you expect to become a member of the group soon, this book will help you get the best out of your air travel experiences.

Why should I need help to take a plane ride? you ask. A seemingly simple activity should not need a guide book. Alas, it is not so simple an activity. The air fare system is mind-boggling; the airports are huge, crowded mazes; the rules and regulations covering air transport are obscure; and air travel itself can be frightening if you don't understand what is going on or what sounds and sensations you can expect to encounter in the air. Customs, immigration, and security checks are time-consuming and often inexplicable processes, especially if you are in a country where you do not speak the language. To minimize the problems that any air traveler can encounter, this chapter clearly explains the procedures you must go through to prepare for and to take a trip. In ten steps you'll learn how to deal with a travel agent, how to apply for a passport, what to do at the airport, and how to deal with customs.

The chapters that follow highlight what you need to know about the major international and domestic airlines, the larger airports, the legal rights of all air travelers, and how to choose the best fare for your trip.

When you have all the available information at your fingertips, you can make sure that your trip goes as well as possible. And if it doesn't, you can make sure you receive the compensation you deserve. Whatever your questions, *Superflier* has the answers. And when you've got the answers, *you're* the travel pro!

"A JOURNEY OF A THOUSAND MILES BEGINS WITH ONE STEP"

Fortunately there are only ten basic steps that you need to get you from your front door to your destination, no matter if it is 100 or 10,000 miles away. These ten steps will remove the mystery and worry from your trip and make you a knowledgeable world traveler before you leave your front door!

STEP ONE: TRAVEL AGENTS

A good travel agent is the key to the successful planning of any trip. He can arrange for all your needs, from passports to theater tickets. A good agent will know about the area you are visiting and will advise you on hotel and sight-seeing services, car rentals—your whole itinerary if you wish. The best part of it all is that except for cables and long-distance calls most of his services are free to you. (He makes his money from commissions paid by the airlines, hotels and other tourist service companies.)

Your job in dealing with any travel agent is twofold. First, you must select an agent who is honest, experienced and knowledgeable. Then you must provide the agent with complete information about your plans, taste and needs. (*Note:* Occasionally, an agent will charge you for "extra services" such as ticket and itinerary changes, visa applications, etc. Ask your agent to tell you precisely what he charges *before* he begins working for you!)

Below are guidelines for choosing and dealing with a travel agent.

WHAT A TRAVEL AGENT DOES

1. Secures air reservations and tickets
2. Gathers information and application forms for passports, visas and inoculations
3. Plans your itinerary, including sight-seeing and cultural activities
4. Provides complete hotel information and reservation services
5. Arranges car rentals
6. Obtains theater and special-events tickets
7. Reserves special services from airlines and airports worldwide such as wheelchairs, special meals on board, pet handling, and special medical needs for handicapped or disabled passengers
8. Arranges for customs' approval of transportation of drugs needed for medical reasons
9. Buys travel, life, cancellation, and baggage insurance
10. Handles any complaints you have about service received while you were traveling

HOW TO CHOOSE A TRAVEL AGENT

1. Ask a friend. As with lawyers, accountants or doctors, there is a wide range of experience, integrity, even specialization, to choose from. If you know people who travel frequently, find out what agent they use. A recommendation based on experience is the best kind.
2. Go only to established agencies. Those that have been in business for many years offer you many benefits. Such agencies are more financially stable. They know their information. They are personally acquainted with hotel and tour managers and airline personnel and can get you favors that a newer agent cannot. For example, their clients can be put on a special "wait list" if they cannot get a confirmed airplane reservation on a

crowded flight. This gives their clients priority over other travelers trying to get on the same flight.

3. Look for the ASTA Logo. The American Society of Travel Agents is a self-policing organization that sets standards for its member agencies. Of course this does not guarantee that the agent is reliable but it is a starting point. (You might get one of the 1,000 special agents who have completed ASTA's rigorous two-year travel agent's course.)
4. Select an agent who specializes in your particular needs. If you are going on an exotic trip, such as a cruise or a safari, go to an agent who knows that field.
5. Don't be afraid to ask your prospective agent questions. Find out if he knows his business. Many agents have limited personal travel experience and haven't bothered to learn the air routes or the fares. Who needs them? Also note if your agent asks *you* pertinent questions.

WHAT DO YOU SAY TO A TRAVEL AGENT?

Hello is a good beginning. But that and a ticket to Tokyo will not assure you of a good trip. Basically, you should tell your agent as much as possible about your tastes, needs and budget. Below is a list of specific points.

1. Set a budget. Know your limits. You may dream of nights in Monte Carlo but you have to be able to pay for your dreams. If your agent knows exactly how much you can spend, then you can purchase the best possible arrangements available to you. Discuss fees with your agent. Most of his services are free but he is entitled to

a fee for special services, such as cables and long-distance calls.

2. Be realistic. If you delay in telling what you want and what you can afford, you lose valuable time. The best prices for all services are available to those who pay well ahead of time. Special air fares and land arrangements must be paid for in advance of scheduled departure.

3. Explain any restrictions you may have. If you can't climb stairs, have special dietary requirements or cannot give up certain amenities, tell the agent immediately. Additionally, if you desire special services, special hotel rooms, car rentals, motorbikes, theater tickets, or anything else, let the agent know immediately. The availability of such special services is often limited.

4. Define the limits of your flexibility. How long can you be gone? If you can be flexible about your stay, you may qualify for discount fares.

5. Sketch out the general type of trip you have in mind. Do you want to travel with a group throughout your entire stay? Do you want complete independence?

When all of the initial information is exchanged, then you should do some homework of your own. Find out what historical, cultural and entertainment centers are in the area you will be visiting. Learn about the customs and the lifestyle. The more knowledgeable you are about your destination, the better time you will have when you reach it.

Note: If for any reason you feel that your travel agent is not providing you with enough information, call the airline you are booked on and double check all your plans. If you are not reassured, tell your agent and take your business elsewhere. Do *not* be a passive traveler!

STEP TWO: PASSPORTS, VISAS AND HEALTH REGULATIONS

Your passport is the single most important item you will carry with you while you are out of the country. Without it you cannot be sure of safe passage. If it is ever lost or stolen, report it immediately to the nearest American embassy or consulate and write the Passport Office, Department of State, Washington, D.C. 20524.

WHERE TO APPLY FOR A PASSPORT

You may apply at the U. S. Department of State passport agencies in Boston, Chicago, Honolulu, Los Angeles, Miami, New Orleans, New York, Philadelphia, San Francisco, Seattle and Washington, D.C.; in your local federal and state courthouse or in specially selected post offices.

WHEN TO APPLY

Apply for your travel papers a few months in advance of your departure. Allow extra time if you need visas.

HOW TO APPLY FOR A PASSPORT

There are two ways to apply for a passport—in person and through the mail. The particular conditions governing each method are explained below.

THROUGH THE MAIL

You may apply and pay for your passport through the mail if: You have a passport that was issued in the last eight years and your previous passport was not issued before you were 18; You are able to submit your old passport with your application; You are not applying for an official or diplomatic passport; You do not wish to include a member of your family on your passport.

If you meet these requirements, get your local passport office to send you form DSP-82. Fill it out and return it to the office along with: your old passport, a $10 check or money order, and two identical, full face photos 2'' x 2'' signed on the front left-hand side and on the back. The image size can be no smaller than one inch and no larger than 1⅜ inches.

IN PERSON

You must apply for your passport in person if: You have never had a passport before and are over 12 years of age; You are unable to submit your old passport with your application; You have a passport that is more than eight years old; You wish to include a family member on your passport; You have lost your passport.

Fee: $13 payable by check, cash or money order. State court offices that act as passport offices must be paid with two separate checks or sums: $10 is for the passport and is payable to the U.S. Passport Office; $3 is a processing fee and is payable to the state.

Application forms are available at the passport office or may be sent away for and filled out at home. For an application, write to your regional passport office and request form DSP-11 and all other information on passports. You can find your nearest passport office in the white pages of your telephone directory under U.S. Government, Department of Passport and Immigration. In smaller communities, it may be necessary to travel to your local county seat to obtain information.

IDENTIFICATION REQUIREMENTS

When you have determined that you must apply for your passport in person, you will need to bring the following pieces of identification with you: Previously issued passport (if you have one); or Birth certificate, original or certified copy only; plus Two full face photos, no older than 6 months. Color is acceptable. Size must be 2″ x 2″ and the image size can be no smaller than one inch and no larger than 1⅜ inches, signed on the front left-hand side and the back.

Note: Your passport office states that your husband, wife, minor children, stepchildren, adopted children, minor brothers or sisters may appear on your passport photo if a joint passport is to be issued. *Animals* may not be included in the photo even if they are traveling with you. Makes you wonder what kinds of pictures passport offices must get!

PROBLEMS OF IDENTITY

There are many small snags that can pop up when you are applying for a passport. You should not panic. If you cannot supply the necessary information to the passport office, they will make every effort to help you obtain a passport. The following list of problems that arise frequently will help you find the solution to your particular problem.

If you have a *delayed birth certificate,* one that was issued more than a year after your birth, you must be able to prove that the certificate was issued with strong corroborating evidence or you must follow the steps for those who have no certificate.

If you do *not have a birth certificate,* you must be able to prove your claim of citizenship with some of the following supporting evidence: baptismal certificate, certificate of circumcision, hospital birth record, affidavits from people who have personal knowledge of your birth, early census records, school records, newspaper files, or insurance records.

All evidence must be presented in original or certified copy.

If you were *born outside* the United States, you must be able to show at least one of the following forms: consular report of birth form FS-240; certification of birth form FS–545 or DS–1350; certificate of citizenship.

Note: If none of the above evidence is available, you should supply the following evidence: your foreign birth certificate, evidence of your parents' U.S. citizenship, an affidavit from your parents, showing the dates when they were living outside the U.S.

If you are a *naturalized citizen,* you are required to submit the following identification: certification of naturalization; or if you acquired citizenship through your parents, you should show either a certificate of naturalization or your parents' certificates of naturalization, your foreign birth certificate and proof of your legal admission to the U.S.

Special Cases—The following cases are most particular. If you have any questions about special conditions, call your local passport office.

Women married before September 22, 1922, and women married to aliens ineligible for citizenship before March 3, 1931, should make special inquiry to the passport office.

Dual nationals are warned that the second country of citizenship may claim legal jurisdiction over a traveler once inside the country's boundaries. Dual nationals may be subject to military induction, taxes, etc., and should check with the country's consulate here in the U.S. before venturing abroad.

VISAS

A visa is permission granted by a government to an alien to enter the country for a specific and limited length of time. It is usually shown as a stamp on your passport. The visa rules are very different for each country. In general, however, Western European countries do *not* require a visa for stays of less than three months. Elsewhere the rules are varied and can change without notice.

Visas are your responsibility. You are required to find out what is needed and obtain proper documents. Many countries require weeks to process your application, some require payment, some change requirements frequently. To help you plan a smooth trip, write the Passport Office and request "Visa Requirements of Foreign Governments" Form M–264.

Use this brochure as a general guide, but always contact the consular officials in Washington who represent the country of your destination to get up-to-date facts.

Note: Although there is great emphasis on obtaining visas before you depart the U.S., it is possible to get visas while abroad. If, for example, you are in London and decide you want to go to Prague, you may go to the Czech embassy and apply for a visa. It is sometimes more difficult to get a visa under such circumstances but, if impulse directs you to a country requiring a visa, at least give it a try!

IMMUNIZATION

Today there are far fewer health requirements for travelers than there were even a few years ago. There are still several areas of the world where cholera, smallpox, malaria and other such diseases are a danger. It is sometimes advisable to get inoculated against these diseases, even if it is not required by law, if you are traveling in potentially infected areas. Check with your doctor.

For return to the United States, a smallpox inoculation certificate is required only if the traveler had been in a country that reported an incidence of smallpox within the last 14 days.

International requirements are available through your local health department. A travel agent is able to obtain all necessary information for you. The document, Form PHS 731, on which the record of your inoculations must be entered by your doctor, should be kept with your passport. It will be checked at all borders where such health regulations are in effect.

Note: The most complete manual of all travel requirements (passport, visa, health and currency restrictions) is *The Travel Information Manual,* published by a 15-member IATA group. It is a monthly book of enormous detail and may be obtained by writing to Travel Information Manual, P.O. Box 7627, Amsterdam International Airport, The Netherlands, or by asking one of the following airlines for a copy: Aerolineas Argentinas, Air France, CP Air, Iberia, Japan Air Lines, JAT, KLM, Lufthansa, Olympic Airways, Qantas, Sabena, SAS, Swissair, TWA or Varig.

STEP THREE: TICKETING—PURCHASE, RECONFIRMATION AND CANCELLATION

If you have used a travel agent to plan your trip, you *should not* have to worry about the details of ticketing and reconfirmation. However, it is always important to know how it is done so that you can make sure your agent has followed the proper procedures. If you have made your reservations on your own, then you alone are responsible for making sure all your plans go smoothly. You must know what to do and how to do it.

TICKETING

Whenever you deal with the airlines, always make a note of the name of the person with whom you have spoken. If you make a reservation, reconfirm a reservation or change your original plans, you need to be able to prove that you have done *your* job in case the airlines fail at theirs. No complaint, no claim of mistreatment can be truly effective if you cannot remember with whom you spoke. If possible, have your oral communications confirmed by a written letter from the airlines. When it is not possible, make careful note of all your oral exchanges.

Payment for tickets may be made in cash, check or credit card. If you get a refund for a ticket, it will be in the same currency in which it was paid. For example, if you charge your ticket, a refund is made to your credit card, not to you in cash.

Tickets are nontransferable. It is not legal for one person to use another's ticket.

Lost tickets are your responsibility. The airlines will not give a refund for lost or stolen tickets until they have time to make sure the ticket is not used. This usually takes up to 120 days. Therefore you cannot use the money with which you paid for the first ticket to purchase a replacement. You must buy an additional fare and hope to receive a refund on the first ticket at a later date. If the ticket is used by someone, you are liable for it and do not qualify for a refund.

SPECIAL SERVICES
AVAILABLE UPON REQUEST

The airlines provide many special services that are available only when requested prior to departure, usually at the time your ticket reservation is made.

Handicapped persons should make sure that they discuss their medical needs in detail with their travel agent or airline ticket clerk when they make a reservation. Wheelchair service is provided at all airports by the airlines but they usually need 24 hours' notice to make sure one is available. Other more specialized medical needs should be arranged at least a week ahead of time.

Special food service is available from all airlines for those with dietary, religious, health or personal restrictions. Make requests for special meals at least 24 hours before the scheduled departure of your flight and preferably when you make your reservation. When reconfirming your ticket, always reconfirm special service requests.

Seat preferences may be expressed on all flights, even those domestic flights that do not allow seat reservations. If, for example, you want a seat on the aisle in a nonsmoking section of the plane, you may ask the airline to note that with your reservation. When you arrive at the boarding gate (and you should be at least 20 minutes early), the boarding attendants will have a record of your request and make every effort to accommodate you.

Seat reservations may be made on some transcontinental domestic flights and on intercontinental flights at the time you make your ticket reservation.

Children below the age of nine are not always allowed to travel alone. Some airlines provide for escort service for children, others require adult accompaniment. You should always check ahead of time to see how the airline deals with these young passengers.

Medical restrictions do exist. For example, pregnant women are requested to supply notes from doctors, authorizing them to fly if they are in the last two months of their pregnancy. These requirements vary from airline to airline and should be checked carefully.

RECONFIRMATION OF YOUR RESERVATION

This procedure is simple and sensible. All you have to do is call the reservations number listed on your ticket and inform the airline that you do intend to use your ticket as planned.

DOMESTIC

Flights within the continental United States *do not* have to be reconfirmed. However, it is not a bad idea to call the airline about two days before you are scheduled for departure and make sure that it does, in fact, have your reservation logged in the computer. Many unhappy surprises could be avoided at the airport if this extra precaution were taken more often. Ask the airline employee to make a note that you called and reconfirmed your flight. Make sure you get *his* name.

Note: If you are flying to several cities within the U.S. and you decide to cancel one leg of your trip, be careful! Often the cancellation of one portion will cause the rest of the trip to be canceled. This happens if the computer erases all information under your name. If you are flying on several airlines, this is particularly common. As a precaution, reconfirm all segments of the trip that follow the segment that you cancel.

INTERNATIONAL

International flights *must* be reconfirmed or the reservation will be canceled. The law requires that you reconfirm at least 72 hours before the scheduled departure of your flight.

Note: When traveling abroad, you must reconfirm your return flight separately from the one on which you arrived. It is best to reconfirm immediately upon arrival at your destination. The requirement is that it be reconfirmed at least 72 hours prior to your scheduled departure.

Note: Whenever possible get reconfirmation in writing from the airline. If that is not possible, make a note of the date, time and name of the person with whom you spoke when you reconfirmed.

CANCELLATION

Cancellation can mean several things: you cancel your flight, the airline cancels your flight or you just don't show up for your reservation. There are specific rules governing each circumstance.

DOMESTIC

Flights within the continental U.S. have no cancellation restrictions on the passenger. You can call up and cancel at any time. You can even not show up without notifying the airline, and get a complete refund on the unused ticket. It is best to notify the airline, however, because airlines use the "No-Show" habit as a rationalization for overbooking—that is, for selling more tickets than there are seats available on a flight.

INTERNATIONAL

International flights on U.S. carriers operate under the same rules as domestic flights. But non-U.S. airlines operating *outside* the U.S. may have their own rules. In certain instances both no-shows and cancellations that are made at the last minute are subject to penalties. It is not possible to get a complete refund on your unused ticket. Whenever you are flying abroad on a foreign airline, ask about their cancellation policy before you buy your ticket. The amount you are penalized varies from airline to airline.

CHARTER FLIGHTS

Now that charters have become a common method of air travel, more and more people are confronting the confusing and harsh passenger-cancellation penalties that exist on such flights.

Charter flights have penalties ranging from a nominal fee to the entire cost of the ticket. This varies depending on when you cancel and what kind of charter it is. Most charters in the U.S. have a minimum $50 penalty fee, and international charters tend to hit you for anything—up to the entire ticket price. Always read the cancellation clause before you sign a charter contract.

The reason that there are cancellation penalties on charter flights is that they depend on a full load of passengers to make money. Unlike regular flights with higher prices, a charter depends exclusively on volume.

Note: Cancellation insurance is available. This insurance is sold at the same time you buy your charter ticket. For a nominal fee, you can protect yourself in case you are unable to keep your reservation. You should always buy cancellation insurance.

Unforeseen events can interrupt and spoil your plans. With cancellation insurance you can avoid financial problems. The cost is around $15.

Note: Cancellation insurance does *not* cover you if you are forced to cancel your flight because of a flare-up of a medical condition that you had before you purchased the cancellation insurance. Such ailments as chronic heart disease, etc., would not be covered by the insurance.

What if your air travel plans are disrupted by the airline or charter company? What if they cancel the flight right out from under you? Before increased government supervision came into effect, you might have had a hard time getting a refund. That is not the case any longer (except if the charter company goes bankrupt). But a refund, even if prompt, will not protect you from having to buy a more expensive ticket. If you purchase cancellation insurance for such circumstances, you will be paid *the difference* between the discount fare you initially paid and the new air fare you have to buy as a replacement. Insurance is available from travel agents, airlines and insurance desks in airports.

STEP FOUR: BAGGAGE REGULATIONS AND PACKING TIPS

There are now *new* rules for free baggage allowance. The old rules were very simple weight requirements that applied worldwide. The new requirements are based on the *size*, not the weight of your baggage. Although the new rules were made because consumers complained about the restrictive nature of the old weight requirements, one Pan Am representative did admit that the new rules were adopted in part because "there is a revenue source involved." Oh, brother! What that means is that somehow the airlines will be making more money from the new regulations. When we consumers complain, we had better be more specific!

The new rules are very confusing. We present them here as they are written, with a warning that you should always ask your airline ticket agent to explain the precise rules that apply to you when you make your reservation.

DOMESTIC FREE BAGGAGE ALLOWANCE REGULATIONS

CARRY-ON LUGGAGE

Each ticketed passenger may *carry on* various bags as long as they do *not* exceed 45 inches in *total* size. The size is determined by adding the length and width and depth of each bag. Some airlines are equipped with large on-board storage compartments and will allow additional carry-on luggage. Always check with the airline at the time you make your reservation to find out what is available. For a list of standard carry-on baggage see page 28.

CHECKED LUGGAGE

Each ticketed passenger may check *two* bags. One bag can measure no more than 62 inches, the second no more than 52 inches. (The size is determined by adding the length and width and depth of the bag.) In addition, no one suitcase can weigh more than 70 pounds.
Note: The regulations are the same for first-class and coach passengers.

INTERNATIONAL FREE BAGGAGE ALLOWANCE REGULATIONS

FIRST-CLASS

Passengers traveling first-class internationally may check two bags. Neither bag can measure more than 62 inches.

(The size is determined by adding the length to the width to the depth of the bag.)

Passengers traveling first-class internationally may carry on *any number of bags*, so long as they do not total more than 45 inches in size. Check with the airline when you make your reservation to find out if additional storage compartments are available on your flight. If so, additional carry-on items may be accepted. Always ask!

COACH CLASS

Passengers traveling coach class internationally may check *two* bags. The *combined* measurements of these bags may not exceed 106 inches when measured by adding the width to the depth to the length. No one suitcase may be larger than 62 inches.

Passengers traveling coach class internationally may carry-on various bags or items as long as they do *not* total more than 45 inches in total size. Remember to check with your airline when you make your reservation to find out what kind of on-board storage compartments are available. If there is ample storage, you may be able to bring more carry-on items on the plane. Always ask!

CHILDREN

Children paying at least 50 percent of an adult regular fare have the same baggage allowance as an adult.

INFANTS

Infants who pay at least 10 percent of an adult regular fare have the right to check one bag no larger than 39 inches, plus one collapsible stroller.

Note: These regulations apply to U.S. airlines and foreign airlines *departing from the U.S.* In many countries the old weight requirements still apply. In some circumstances the unwitting passenger can depart from the U.S. with all baggage meeting required *size limits*, but on returning to the U.S. *on the same airline*, he can be hit with huge *over-*

weight charges, because different rules apply at point of departure. Again, ask your airline *before* you pack.

ACCEPTABLE CARRY-ON ITEMS

The following list is a general outline of the kinds of items that may be carried on board. They are not subject to maximum baggage regulations. If you have any questions about specific items, check with your travel agent or airline reservation clerk. You may carry handbags, overcoats, umbrellas and canes, cameras and binoculars, reading material, folding wheelchairs, etc.

SPECIAL RULES FOR CHECKED BAGGAGE

The following list is for irregular luggage. All the pieces are considered 55 inches in dimension regardless of their actual size. They count as one of the two free bags that you are allowed. Included are one sleeping roll or bag, one knapsack or backpack, one pair of skis with boots and poles, one golf bag with shoes, one duffel bag, or one musical instrument that is not longer than 39 inches in any one direction (it will be regarded as a 39-inch bag, no matter what the other dimensions are).

Pets do not qualify for free baggage allowance.

EXCESS BAGGAGE CHARGE

The new excess baggage charges are complicated and inconsistently applied. We provide an outline of the rules but urge you to contact your airline representative if you think your bags will be oversized. If you are over the limit, repack!
Note: Since the bags are evaluated by size, it is possible that you will not be penalized for two large bags that contain exactly the same items as three smaller bags. Try to make the inconsistencies of the law work to your advantage!

DOMESTIC

Domestic excess baggage charges are straightforward. Each bag that is larger than acceptable dimensions (or any bag over two) is charged $6. However, the airlines are not consistent, and you may find you are not charged from your point of departure but have to pay on your return trip. The airline ticket clerks have authority to decide if you will be charged or not.

If your oversized or extra bag weighs more than 70 pounds, you are subject to additional fines. See the international section that follows for a detailed explanation.

INTERNATIONAL

International excess baggage charges are very complicated. The following examples give the charges for transporting one extra bag between the west coast of the U.S. and specific international destinations. Distance is a factor in determining the charge but it is not the only factor as you will see below.

From the West Coast to: Japan, $55; Hong Kong, $65; Australia, $80; India, $90.

Note: If you are flying west from Hawaii or Alaska, *subtract* $10 from the charge to the above destinations. However, if you are flying from Alaska to India or Australia, *add* $5. If you are departing from an airport not on the West Coast, *add* $5.

Overweight baggage (more than 70 pounds per bag) is subject to an extra charge. Bags weighing more than 80 pounds are subject to special rules.

Call the airline and arrange ahead of time for your bag to be weighed when you check in.

Charges for bags weighing more than 80 pounds are determined by charging three times the amounts listed above for the first 45 kilograms (1 kilo = 2.2 pounds). For any weight above 45 kilos, there is an additional charge for each 10 pounds.

Note: You would be much better off dividing your bags' contents between two smaller bags and paying a standard excess baggage charge on one of them than getting involved with this triple-fine business. Another idea—carry on particularly heavy objects.

Note: American Airlines told us they didn't mind one passenger checking through three bags as long as they didn't exceed size and weight limits for two bags. Pan Am said they would not accept that. Our advice? Call the airline or have your travel agent check it out for you.

PACKING TIPS

There are several things that you can do to minimize the risk of loss or damage to your possessions and your baggage. A cautious traveler is often the happiest—when it comes to baggage.

Arrive at the airport early. If you enter the airport at a full run, race through check-in, and leap onto the plane just before it taxis down the runway, your bags will probably be left behind. It takes the bags longer to get to the plane than it takes you.

Mark your bags with some distinctive tape so that you can pick them out in a crowd. So many people have suitcases that look alike.

Have your name and address (preferably business address) on the outside *and* the inside of your bag.

Lock your luggage. It discourages vandalism and makes it easier to tell if your bag has been broken into when you pick it up at the baggage claim area.

Don't overpack your bags. The airlines aren't liable for damage to bags that are overpacked.

BAGGAGE DAMAGE—LIABILITY AND RESTRICTIONS

Airlines are liable for passengers' standard fragile items such as glasses, contacts, one camera per passenger and a reasonable amount of toiletries. (These are items an airline must assume all travelers will have with them.)

However, unusual fragile items such as glass, artwork or antiques should not be packed in your luggage because the airline *may* disclaim responsibility if they are damaged (or lost). The airlines cannot assume responsibility for exceptional contents without prior notice.

If you have fragile items to transport, you are better off leaving them out of your suitcase. Airlines are liable for damage to fragile items *not* carried inside luggage—such as musical instruments or antiques—*unless* you sign a waiver releasing them from responsibility *before* you check the item for transportation.

Airlines *are* responsible for damage to contents when baggage itself is damaged, dented, torn, etc., through negligent abuse.

Airlines *are* responsible for any item still packed in its original factory-sealed carton, container or case.

BAGGAGE RESTRICTIONS

The following items may not be transported in baggage or on your person: compressed gas, acids, alkalies or wet cell batteries, fireworks, lighter fluid (or any flammable fluid), peroxide, poisons, magnetic materials.

EXCESS VALUE BAGGAGE INSURANCE

If you have items worth more than the maximum liability ($750 per person domestic; $9.07 per pound international), be sure you take out additional insurance.

You may purchase it at the airline check-in counter at the airport. Do not be dissuaded by airline personnel who assure you, "There's no need to worry." Their assurance is not worth one cent and they cannot promise you anything. The cost for excess value insurance is 10 cents per $100 of excess value for domestic flights and 15 cents per $100 of excess value for international flights. Items valued up to $25,000 are insurable.

STEP FIVE: AIRPORT CHECK-IN

It is very important that you check with your airline or travel agent to find out what the check-in time requirements are at the various airports from which you will be departing. In the

U.S. there are uniform requirements for all domestic and international flights, as explained below. In the rest of the world the regulations vary according to each airline and airport. If, for example, you are flying on Lufthansa from Addis Ababa to Frankfurt, you should check the Lufthansa timetable to see what the specific check-in requirements are for those airports. (It is 60 minutes.) Failure to observe the check-in time limitations in the U.S. and abroad can result in the cancellation of your reservation.

CHECK-IN PROCEDURES

When you arrive at the airport, you proceed immediately to the airline's ticket counter.

At the counter you inform the airline you have arrived for the flight and (hopefully) they have your name on their passenger list.

Baggage is checked at this time and you are given a claim ticket that you must keep in order to retrieve your bags at your destination.

If you are checking your baggage through from your original flight to a connecting one, make sure that your bags are properly tagged when you check in.

All baggage is required by law to have an outside identification tag. These are available from the airlines at the check-in counters. If you can put an office address and phone number on your tag, do so in order to prevent clever burglars from learning your home address. (The police warn that some people hang out in airports and collect the addresses of departing travelers.)

You can arrange to pick up your ticket at the airport check-in counter. However, when you make your reservation, find out how far in advance you have to pick up your ticket. In some cases tickets will not be held if you don't pick them up at least an hour before the scheduled departure of the flight.

DOMESTIC FLIGHTS

In the U.S. you are required by law to check in no less than five minutes before the scheduled departure of your flight.

Failure to do so can result in the cancellation of your reservation. These days with overbooking, busy check-in counters, prolonged security checks and remote boarding areas, this is usually cutting it much too close.

Note: Many domestic airlines have stricter time limits than the law specifies. These stricter deadlines are shown in their timetables. Check this information carefully. As a general rule you should try to arrive at the check-in counter at least 20 minutes before the scheduled departure of your domestic flight.

INTERNATIONAL FLIGHTS

In the U.S. you are required by law to check in no less than 20 minutes before the scheduled departure of an international flight. Failure to do so can result in the cancellation of your reservation.

Note: Here again many airlines have stricter requirements than the law requires. Check the airline's timetable so you don't unnecessarily jeopardize your reservation.

Note: Overbooking is a serious problem! The airlines are often guilty of selling more tickets than there are seats on any one plane. Therefore there are often people with confirmed reservations who do not get a seat on the plane. To avoid having that happen to you, always *arrive early*. The seats are usually given out on a first-come, first-served basis. If the flight is oversold, promptness is your only defense. (For complete details on what to do if you are a victim of overbooking, see chapter two.)

SEAT SELECTION

Whether you can make a seat reservation or not (on short-distance flights within the U.S. you cannot), here are some tips on how to select the safest and most comfortable seat.

Each airline makes its own particular seating arrangements according to the type of craft, the route flown, and the facilities on board. For example, on Eastern's shuttle service and on many other airlines' high-volume-discount-ticket routes, seats are added to maximize profits. On many domestic 747s, however, seats are removed, aisles widened, etc.

To familiarize you with seating charts, we have included American's 747 Luxury Liner seating chart. Many airlines now provide seating charts on request. Just ask.

SAFETY

It is hard to separate superstition from fact when it comes to choosing a safe seat. We pass the following ideas along without comment (almost)!

—In a nose-first crash, seats in the back of the plane are the safest; seats in front, well . . .

—Most deaths in plane crashes result from asphyxiation; therefore it would be better to sit next to an exit.

—Exits are often over the wings, which are full of huge tanks of flammable fuel. It might be dangerous to be so near the fuel.

—The front of the plane is farthest away from the fuel tanks and might be safest.

A complete circle! You decide for yourself!

COMFORT

It is no easier to choose a comfortable seat than a safe one. Below we list some of the factors you might want to consider when you make your choice. You will have to decide what your particular needs are.

—Airplanes are supposed to be more stable and, therefore, smoother riding near the midsection.

—Airplanes are quieter in the forward sections.

—The first row in any seating section generally has more legroom than the other rows.

—Window seats are preferable for privacy and a view.

—Aisle seats are preferable for mobility but are subject to constant contact with people going up and down the aisles.

—Deplaning is fastest in the front or near any regular exit, but, unless your baggage is on board with you, you will lose that time waiting for your baggage. If you need to deplane quickly to meet a connecting flight, arrange with

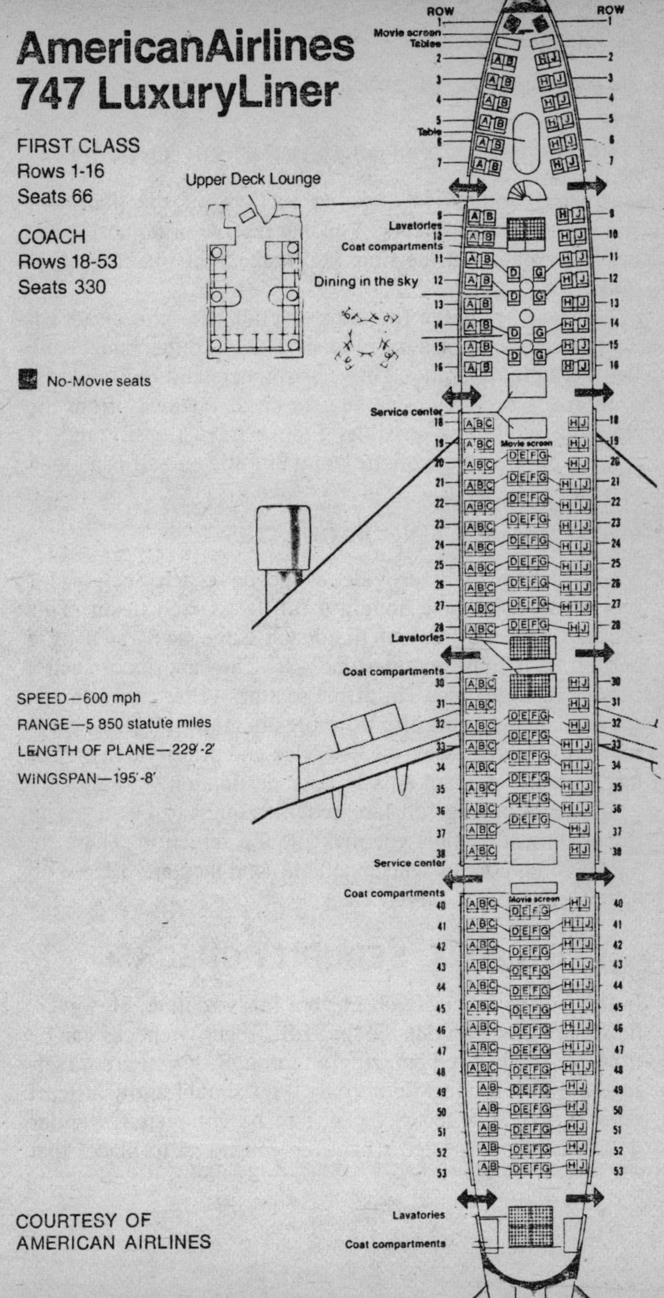

AmericanAirlines
747 LuxuryLiner

FIRST CLASS
Rows 1-16
Seats 66

COACH
Rows 18-53
Seats 330

No-Movie seats

SPEED—600 mph
RANGE—5 850 statute miles
LENGTH OF PLANE—229'-2'
WINGSPAN—195'-8'

COURTESY OF
AMERICAN AIRLINES

Upper Deck Lounge

ROW
ROW
Movie screen
Tables
Table
Lavatories
Coat compartments
Dining in the sky
Service center
Movie screen
Lavatories
Coat compartments
Coat compartments
Service center
Coat compartments
Movie screen
Lavatories
Coat compartments

the flight attendant beforehand and you will be sped on your way.

SMOKING AND NONSMOKING SECTION

Airlines now provide separate sections of the plane for smokers and nonsmokers. You can reserve or request a seat in either section at the time you make your ticket reservation.

Nonsmokers in the first-class sections are at a disadvantage because the seating area is always rather small and there is little separation between smokers and nonsmokers.

In coach sections remember to sit as far away from the smoking section as possible. Smoke travels easily and, if you are close to the section, you will find yourself in a cloud of smoke.

SPECIAL SEATING FACILITIES

Many airlines now provide a special coach section for passengers who have bought a full-fare coach ticket. This section is in the front of the coach cabin, separated by a curtain. It is most common in 747s. The benefits of such a service include quiet, child-free seating, faster check-in at a special counter in the airport, more attention and better service on the plane, faster meal service and priority delivery of baggage to the claim area at your destination.

If you're paying full-fare coach, request to be seated in this section at the time you make your reservation. There are a limited number of seats available, and they are offered on a first-asked, first-served basis.

STEP SIX: SECURITY CHECKS

In this country security checks are fairly routine. However, if you are traveling outside the U.S., security checks can be time-consuming and amazingly thorough. If you are traveling to or are in the Middle East, you should allow at least one hour for the security check to be completed. Similar delays can be expected whenever you travel to places that are experiencing political or military disorders. The airlines do not assume any responsibility for delays encountered by their passengers. Be sure to give yourself enough time to catch your plane.

THE PROCESS

The procedure in this country is usually consistent from airport to airport. The security checkpoint is in the concourse that connects the ticket counter lobby to the gate.

—You will be stopped there.

—Give your carry-on bags to the security personnel.

—The bags will be passed through an electronic scanner, much like an X ray.

—Sometimes bags and purses will be opened and searched.

—You will have to walk through a metal detector that looks like a free-standing door frame. Do not be surprised if you are asked to remove objects from your pockets. That's routine.

Note: Be patient with this process. It is for your own protection. Now! On to the boarding gate.

STEP SEVEN: AT THE BOARDING GATE

The boarding or departure gate is a waiting area with seats for the passengers on a particular flight. At the gate you must often complete your check-in procedures. Seat assignments, boarding passes and special assistance to the disabled are often handled at this point.

THE PROCESS

Arrive early. Try to give yourself as much time as possible for the entire check-in and security process so that you are not rushed when you get to the gate. Reservations are not honored for those who arrive at the boarding gate late.

—Boarding attendants will have you line up to receive boarding passes or to make seat assignments if that was not done at the check-in counter.

—Flight attendants and boarding personnel are available to handle any problems you may have.

Note: Remember check-in requirements are often stricter than the law requires. Always ask airline personnel for specific requirements when you make your ticket reservation.

STEP EIGHT: BOARDING AND IN-FLIGHT ROUTINE

The following list covers what you will encounter during your flight. If at any time you are in need of assistance or if you need specific information not covered in this section, the gate and flight attendants are always at your service. Do not hesitate to seek their advice, reassurance or assistance.

THE PROCESS

—Boarding will be announced to you as you wait in the lounge area at the gate. Have your boarding pass and/or ticket handy.

—Planes are boarded through enclosed walkways that extend from the gate to the plane or by exterior stairways that are brought up alongside the plane and are approached by walking outside on the tarmac.

—At the door of the plane you present your boarding pass and ticket to the flight attendant.

—The attendant will direct you toward your seat. On most aircraft, *rows* are numbered from front to back, begining with No. 1. Seats are identified alphabetically from side to side. The seat numbers are located on the overhead compartment, on the seat arm, or over the windows. (See sample seating chart p. 35.)

—Stow your carry-on luggage under the seat in front of you or in the overhead storage compartments. Hanging bags or coats can usually be hung up by the flight attendant in the front of the cabin section.

—Observe the "fasten your seat belt" and "no smoking" signs when they are turned on.

—Flight attendants will demonstrate how to use the oxygen masks in case there is a loss of cabin pressure. They will point out the emergency exits and the location of the flotation jackets.

—The seat-belt and no-smoking signs are turned off after takeoff. You may then walk around. However, keep your seat belt fastened whenever you are in your seat. The plane can encounter "turbulence." This can happen in clear or cloudy weather. It is not unlike a wave. It has as little effect on a plane as a wave does on an ocean liner, but you can be tossed about. So keep your seat belt fastened.

—Meals are served at appropriate times. There is no way to predict which seats will be served first. If your flight is very short or falls between mealtimes, a snack may be served. Liquor is free to first-class passengers and available for a fee to coach passengers.

—Assistance can be summoned at anytime by signaling the attendant. A console above your seat will have a small button that you pull to summon the attendant. An adjustable light and an air jet are also on the console. Attendants can supply you with magazines, blankets, pillows, etc., upon request.

—Consoles located on the arm on the seat contain the movie and radio headphone jacks and the ashtray and seat-adjustment lever. Music and movie headphones are available on most long distance flights. There is a charge of $2 on domestic flights and $2.50 on international flights.

—Bathroom facilities on jets vary, and most have outlets for electric shavers and some provide soap, towels, aftershave, etc. On jumbo jets, the lines to the bathrooms can be very long, particularly after a meal is served. Try to plan ahead so that you are not caught in the crunch!

THE SENSATIONS OF FLIGHT

You can expect to experience some or all of the following:

—The steady stream of air you hear is air circulating through the cabin and air coming from the vents above your seat. It will cease while engines are being started; the additional air is used to turn the air-driven engine starters.

—As the airplane taxis, you hear a rumbling and humming sound as the flaps on the wings are lowered for takeoff. After takeoff, you'll hear the same kind of noise as the flaps are retracted. Again as the airplane approaches the airport and starts slowing down, the flaps will be lowered. There'll be grinding-and-thud noise. At touchdown, panels on the wing rise.

—After takeoff, you will hear a clank and a grinding noise. It's caused by the wheel brakes that stop wheel rotation and by retraction of the wheels.

—During flight the wingtips rise and fall slightly for the same reason that skyscrapers sway in the wind—a little "give" reduces stress on the frame.

GETTING READY TO LAND

Landing forms, customs declarations and immigration forms will be distributed to you sometime during your international flight. Fill these out and have them ready for presentation to the authorities when you land. Your flight attendant will answer any questions you might have. Check the section on customs and immigration for complete information about rules and regulations.

—Descent begins quite a distance from the airport. The "fasten your seat belt" and "no-smoking" signs will be reactivated. You will have to remove any trays from your seat and put your seat back in an upright position. At some point during the descent, the landing gear will be lowered.

—Deplaning will take place after the plane has come to a full stop and the stairway or ramp has been brought up to the plane. Until that time you are requested to remain in your seat, with your seat belt fastened. It never happens. Everyone begins to scramble. But be patient. Sometimes it is quite a distance from the plane to the terminal, so wait and see what procedure is being followed before you charge down the aisle and then have to stand for 20 minutes.

—If you are meeting a connecting flight, make sure you have all your carry-on luggage assembled before the plane begins its descent. Sit near an exit and ask the flight attendant to help you get off the plane quickly.

YOUR HEALTH EN ROUTE

Today's airplanes are comfortable, pressurized craft. You should not experience any physical discomfort while in the air. However, certain symptoms of nervousness and of change of air pressure can occur. Below is a survey of the most common physical responses.

Aerosinusitis: This is a painful condition that is caused by the changes in atmospheric pressure around you and the resulting imbalance between your sinus pressure and the outside atmosphere. Aircraft are pressurized at about 7,000 feet, so flying at 30,000 feet is like visiting the Rockies outside of Denver, Colorado. Although aerosinusitis does not occur under normal conditions, it can develop if you have a sinus infection, a head cold or allergies. If you are flying when you have any of these conditions, check with your doctor first. He will give you medication or advise you not to fly.

Nausea: This feeling, so common when planes were unpressurized, is unusual these days. Known as "air sickness," it most commonly results from nervousness or turbulence. Stay calm and summon the flight attendant. There is always a heavy paper bag in the seat pocket in front of you if you become sick and cannot make it to the lavatory. Sometimes the flight attendants will distribute hard candy before departure. If you suck on it during take-off, it may quiet your stomach.

Clogged Ears: This is the most common airplane malady. It comes from the rapid change in pressure during take-off and descent, and feels the same way it does when you take a very fast elevator up to high floors. It can be helped by yawning or by chewing gum.

Jet Lag: This universal malady affects all long-distance travelers to one degree or another. It is caused by the upsetting of the natural body clock—the circadian rhythm. This is the term used to describe the body's natural clock, which operates on a 24-hour cycle. Whenever you travel from one time zone to another, your body clock will maintain the sense of time it had in its original locale. It can adjust to another time zone only over a period of time. In order to minimize the effects of jet lag, follow the suggestions listed below.

—Avoid heavy eating during travel. Any extra load that is put on your body's internal functions slows down its ability to adjust.

—Do not drink. All the body's organs are functioning at low levels of efficiency anyway, and the liver, which processes the alcohol in the blood, will be further slowed down. Not only will the alcohol remain in your blood longer than usual, but you will feel more intoxicated than usual. One drink at 10,000 feet has the effect of two on the ground.

—Reserve time the first day you arrive in a new time zone to rest. Do not try to conduct important business immediately upon arriving in another time zone (particularly if the local time is four or more hours different from your home time). See Appendix A for time zone differences.

—Limit smoking. Smoking at high altitudes robs your blood of the available oxygen. Since there is less air pressure, there is less available oxygen at higher altitudes. Smoking can cause increased feelings of fatigue and make jet lag worse.

STEP NINE: CUSTOMS AND IMMIGRATION

Once you have deplaned from your aircraft, you proceed immediately to the immigration area. There you will show your passport, visa and immunization papers, plus the landing card you have filled out on the plane. Always keep a copy of the landing card that is given you. Some countries require it when you exit.

No matter whether you are entering the U.S. or another country, you will always pass through immigration first, then collect your baggage and then proceed to customs. How each of these steps is handled varies from country to country. In Europe there is not much checking of baggage when you cross the borders between countries. Elsewhere, officials dump out the entire contents of all your bags without warning.

Do not try to outsmart the customs officials and *never* agree to take a package across the border for a stranger.

THE PROCESS

—Immigration authorities will check your passport, visa and other applicable papers. They will stamp your passport with a ''stamp of entry'' and give you a copy of your landing card. Keep them both together in a safe place!

—In most foreign countries, you will be asked to give the address of where you are staying. Hotels will ask for your passport when you check in. They will return it to you after they have notified the police of your presence.

—The baggage area is your second stop after immigration. There you will get your luggage (hopefully) and proceed to the customs area.

—Customs officials will ask you for the ''declaration card'' that you filled out on the plane. They may also inspect your baggage at that time. When entering the U.S. from abroad, you are asked to declare what you have purchased abroad only if it is worth more than $300. As with all customs services, they may inspect your bags if they doubt the truth of your declaration. The procedures followed by customs officials vary greatly abroad. Be prepared for the irrational and stay calm.

—Duty is determined by the official. You must pay what he says. Payment is made either to him or to a cashier who records payment on a receipt. You may receive your baggage only after payment is made.

U.S. CUSTOMS
REGULATIONS—DECLARATIONS

The law requires that all persons entering the U.S. must declare: all articles acquired abroad. Written declaration is required if total value of all articles exceeds $300; all gifts that you have purchased for people other than yourself; any repairs or alterations to your personal goods that were done while abroad; all items that you have bought for resale or for use in your own business.

Oral declaration: If you have *not* purchased more than $300 worth of goods, you may complete only the identification portion of your "declaration card" and state orally that you have nothing to declare.

Written declaration: If you *have* purchased more than $300 worth of goods while abroad, you must fill out the declaration card entirely. More than one quart of alcohol and more than 100 cigars must also be declared and cannot come under the oral declaration provision.

Family declaration: If a family has traveled abroad together and returns together, they may pool their duty-free limit. A family of four is, therefore, entitled to $1,200 worth of duty-free purchases no matter who in the family they belong to.

Special Regulations: There are several special regulations controlling the importing of specific items in the U.S. You should know about them before you go. They can save you money and time.

—*Generalized System of Preferences (GSP)* is the fancy name given to a program that allows products from certain underdeveloped countries to be imported into this country *duty-free* no matter what their cost. There are 98 countries and 40 dependent territories covered by this provision.

GSP imports must meet certain standards. They must be made or manufactured entirely within the country of purchase. A Certificate of Origin is necessary for items worth more than $250. This is given to you at the shop where you purchased the item. Footwear, most textiles, watches, some electronic products, some glass and steel products are *not* included in this program.

Ask or write Department of the Treasury, U.S. Customs Service, Washington, D.C., 20229, for their brochure "GSP and the Traveler" for a complete list of countries covered.

—*Illegal imports* are subject to confiscation by the customs service without compensation to you for the loss. A list of specific items includes: firearms, biological material, absinthe, lottery tickets, narcotics (if you need narcotics for medical reasons, make sure you travel with a note and prescription from your doctor), obscene publications, switchblades, fruit, vegetables, plants, meats, livestock, poultry or merchandise from North Korea or Cuba or Rhodesia.

—*Endangered species products* are also subject to confiscation without compensation. If you buy a leopard-skin coat while abroad, you will never get it home. There are 425 animals in all that are on the U.S. endangered species list. They range from crocodiles to tortoise shells. If you have any questions about what is endangered, write to: Department of the Interior, "Facts About Federal Wildlife Laws," P.O. Box 19183, Washington, D.C. 21136.

GENERAL TIPS

Film bought abroad must be included in your $300 duty-free limit. U.S. film can be taken with you at no charge.

—Reentry to the U.S. more than once in any 30-day period does *not* entitle you to more than $300 free imports. If you do not use up your full $300 quota on your first trip, you may *not* carry the balance to additional trips. All trips after the first, in any 30-day period, are entitled to only $10 worth of duty-free imports.

—To avoid paying duty more than once on any items that you have imported, retain your duty receipts or (if item was imported under duty-free limit) ask customs official for certification that proves you have already passed through customs with it.

—Keep all sales slips for purchases made abroad.

—Mail purchases home. Do not bring them with you. Gifts purchased abroad may be sent home, duty-free, if they are worth less than $10. Mark outside of package "Unsolicited Gift: Value Under $10."

—Foreign articles bought in the U.S. but taken out of the country can be subject to tax if you do not clear the items with the customs service. Items such as cameras, designer dresses, jewelry and other articles of value should be cleared with customs *before* you leave the U.S. or should be accompanied by their sales slip. To clear such foreign made valuables with the customs service call the service at the international airport nearest you. They can arrange for you to have a customs official see and certify the items before you check in for your flight. This process can take time, so allow extra time in your schedule.

Payment of Duty: If you have to pay a duty charge after you have gone through customs, you may pay in U.S. currency, by personal check or traveler's check. If you pay by traveler's check, the value of the check cannot exceed the amount of duty by more than four percent. For example, you can use a $50 traveler's check to pay duty of $48–50 only. If your duty was less than $48, you would have to use a check of a smaller denomination and pay the balance in cash.

Additional Information: For any additional information and brochures write to Department of the Treasury, U.S. Customs Service, "Know Before You Go," Washington, D.C. 20229. U.S. customs service representatives are located in Frankfurt, Paris, London, Rome, Bonn, Montreal, Mexico City, Tokyo, Taipei and Hong Kong. If you are importing items for resale, or if you have any particularly unusual questions, these representatives can be helpful.

If a customs officer damages your bags during inspection, you will be given compensation. Ask for form SF9-5. (You can get it from any U.S. government office.) Send it to the regional customs office in the state in which the damage occurred.

Special Note: Preclearance is an innovation in customs. Since 1976 passengers traveling to the U.S. from Canada, Bermuda or the Bahamas have been able to go through customs inspection "at point of departure" instead of "point of entry." If you wish to use this service, ask your travel agent, airline or customs office for details.

STEP TEN: TRAVELER'S TIPS

Traveler's Tips: What's going on on the ground?

Here's some special information about what's going on down on the ground—the customs, the accommodations, and the special tourist services that are available. *Note:* See Appendix A for charts on metric conversion, clothing sizes, time zones, and addresses of U.S. embassies and consulates all around the globe!

GENERAL TIPS

Keep all travel papers (tickets, baggage claims, passport, visas, health certificates, etc.) in a handy packet or wallet that is easily accessible at all times. *Never* pack your travel documents in your suitcase. Fines are levied against travelers who arrive at immigration counters without their papers. You do not get your baggage before you go through immigration. You can be deported from some countries for such a mistake.

Do not cash American currency on the black market. You can make a big profit in some countries but the risks are not worth it. You can end up in jail.

Contact U.S. consular or embassy officials if you find yourself in trouble (rightly or wrongly) with the local police. You have the right to contact them even if the police are reluctant to allow you to do so.

If you become destitute while you are abroad, the American government does *not* have to give you money. It does no harm to contact them, however, and see if they can suggest any remedies. It's potluck whether or not they will be helpful or rude.

Crime victims should contact the local U.S. diplomatic facility immediately. Under such circumstances they will help you. They can tell you how to deal with the local police and can provide you with communication services to your home bank so you can have additional funds sent you.

MEDICAL ATTENTION WHILE ABROAD

DON'TS

Don't ask hotel or tour staff employees for recommendations about doctors if you become sick. You cannot be sure they are sending you to a qualified person.

Don't go to a hospital without knowing something about it. University hospitals are a good bet if you must.

Don't rely on sign language. Find someone you can speak to.

DOS

Do plan ahead. Before you leave the U.S., get in touch with a service known as Intermedic. This organization will send you a list (for $5.00) of doctors worldwide who have the education and training to meet standards. Write: Intermedic, 777 Third Avenue, New York, New York 10017.

Do write to another organization that provides a similar list free. IAMAT, 350 Fifth Avenue, Suite 5620, New York, New York 10007.

Do contact your Blue Cross office to get their booklet on medical phrases in many languages.

Do find out if your health care covers you while out of the U.S. Most policies do not. You may purchase a rider for the duration of your trip that will extend the coverage to you.

Do contact the local diplomatic offices of the U.S. if you are abroad and need help. They may not be the best clearinghouse of medical information, but they will know doctors who speak English, and that alone is a major help!

TRAVELING ON A BUDGET

If you are traveling on a limited budget, there is no reason why you can't have an enjoyable trip. Just follow these suggestions and you'll be on your way to an economical, fun-filled holiday.

Go to your local library and look up the addresses of the tourist boards that represent the countries you want to visit.

Contact them for information on all discount and budget services available. They will have lists of good, inexpensive hotels and other kinds of living facilities, discounts on transportation and tips on where to go and what to see.

Plan your trip early. The new air fares offer the lowest prices to those people who can prepay for their tickets and/or accommodations far in advance. The cheapest fares are available only if you pay for them 60 days before the scheduled date of your departure.

Travel during the times of the year when the peak tourist season is over. In Europe the summer months are the peak time, in southern resort areas the winter months are peak. During these times hotels, air fares and all services are more expensive than they are the rest of the year. For complete information about fares and seasons, see chapter five.

—Take to the countryside wherever you travel. The most uniquely native sights and experiences are often available outside the large urban centers. Very special accommodations and low prices are common. You have to do some research to find out about the best of these places but your travel agent should be able to help you.

—Always change your money at a bank or official currency exchange. Hotels and other commercial businesses will not give you the best rate. Why throw money away? If you need cash immediately, there are always currency exchanges at all airports when you arrive. If you wish, you may even arrange for your local American bank to supply you with a few dollars in the domestic currency used in your point of arrival so that you can tip the porters and get a taxi without having to worry about having the right money on you.

—Be honest with yourself. What can you do without? What must you have? How fancy does your hotel have to be for you to be comfortable? Can you give up a private bath? The savings are considerable if you can scale down your requirements only slightly.

—Use public transportation whenever possible. Take advantage of special ''unlimited usage'' passes that are available to tourists in all major European cities. These passes allow the tourist to travel on public transportation as much as necessary for one flat fee.

—Student discounts are still available all over Europe. Eurailpass, intra-European airlines, public transportation, museums, concerts and lodging are all discounted for students. Complete information and international student identification cards are obtainable from the National Student Travel Bureau. Write them at 300 E.40th Street, New York, New York 10016; 2115 S Street N.W., Washington, D.C. 20008; or 1007 Broxton Avenue, Los Angeles, California 90024.

CHAPTER TWO
THE ASSERTIVE TRAVELER

You've done your homework. You know you have obtained the best fare and the best accommodations for your trip. Your travel agent dug out all the obscure information you insisted on; your airline told you exactly what your fare options were; you packed correctly; and you have all your travel documents in hand. That *should* be enough. It's time for a vacation!

But don't think you are going to get off that easily. You have yet to arrive at the airport!

Ah! You say you have your reservation. Reconfirmed even? Well, so does someone else—have *your* reservation, we mean.

You say you have your baggage clearly labeled. Inside and out? So, they'll know where to reach you when the bag ends up in Yankton!

This chapter describes what to do when your plans go wrong. We tell you who runs the show and who looks out for your rights. We tell you what your rights are and offer suggestions on how to see they are observed. We prepare you for dealing with the airlines from a position of strength.

We don't want to scare you but you should be prepared. To minimize the problems caused by disappearing bags and non-existent confirmed reservations, keep the following points in mind. (Then if they fail—read on. The next section tells you what "higher authorities" you can appeal to if you fail to get the airlines to listen to you.)

GENERAL TIPS

Arrive early at the airport. Since many airlines are now selling more reserved seats than are available, the seats sold are actually given out on a first-reservation-checked-in, first-reservation-honored basis. We elaborate on this problem and what you can do if it happens to you on the following pages.

Baggage is less likely to get misrouted if you arrive early enough to allow it to get on your plane ahead of time.

Canceled reservations can occur if you are prevented from arriving at the departure gate by the required time. Anything from a traffic jam to a long security check can cause a delay, so allow time for the unexpected.

Record your ticket number and keep it in a special place, not with your ticket. If your ticket is lost or stolen you have a much better chance of getting a refund if you know the number. It is the only thing the computer understands.

Always reconfirm your flight. It is *required* to reconfirm international flights at least 72 hours before the scheduled time of departure. It is a *good idea* to reconfirm domestic flights to make sure you are properly recorded on the passenger list but it is not required by law.

Cancellation of one segment of a multi-flight trip can endanger all following flights if they are not reconfirmed. This is a common error and although it is not supposed to happen it often does.

Always record the *name* of the airlines employee to whom you spoke when reconfirming your reservation. That way you can deal with a particular individual if there is any mix-up. Try and get record of your reconfirmation in writing whenever time permits.

Excess value baggage insurance is a worthwhile investment. Top liability assumed by airlines for loss or damage of your bags is $750 per passenger. The insurance is 10-15 cents per $100—a minimal cost for peace of mind.

SPECIAL PROBLEMS

This section explores the problems of overbooking and lost, delayed or damaged baggage, and offers suggestions on the best way to assert your air traveler rights.

OVERBOOKING

There is an elementary law of physics that states that no two objects may occupy the same space at the same time. This is taught to every schoolchild. Funny that the airlines never heard of it. How else could you explain the increasing problem of *deliberate overbooking?*

THE PROBLEM

The airlines, in an attempt to have as few empty seats as possible, book extra passengers on their flights to offset any last-minute passenger cancellations and no-shows.

Customers do *not* notify the airlines when they plan to cancel a flight. If they did, the airlines could overbook less of the time.

The airlines feel that they can statistically predict the percentage of no-shows and last-minute cancellations. They believe that they can foretell human behavior. Human behavior is not very predictable; therefore, sometimes there are more passengers than seats.

THE NUMBERS

150,000+ passengers with confirmed reservations are denied boarding every year. That is on U.S. certified airlines alone.

THE LAW

All tickets must now have this statement attached: ''Airline flights may be overbooked, and there is a slight chance that a seat will not be available on a flight for which a person has a confirmed reservation. A person denied boarding a flight may be entitled to compensatory payment. The rules for denied boarding are available at all airport ticket counters.''

Before an airline passenger is denied boarding *against his will*. the airline must seek volunteer passengers who will agree to be bumped in exchange for a payment to be determined by the airline. (It usually amounts to the price of your ticket.)

If there are fewer volunteers than necessary, the airline can arbitrarily deny boarding to as many passengers as necessary. Each airline has its own policy of ''boarding priorities.'' This means each airline has its own way of selecting those passengers it will bump. The Civil Aeronautics Board now requires that ''boarding priorities'' be revealed upon request. (The standard method of bumping seems to be to bump late check-ins, late arrivals at boarding gate, and passengers who paid discounted fares.)

Passengers who are involuntarily denied boarding now receive compensation in two ways:—payment equal to the full value of your ticket is made immediately when you are bumped (minimum payment—$37.50; maximum payment —$200) and additional payment is made if you are not *reseated* on a plane that arrives at your destination within two hours (on domestic flights) or four hours (on international flights) of your originally scheduled arrival. Payment is equal to your ticket price and is not less than $37.50 or more than $200.

Therefore: if you are both denied boarding, and not *reseated* within the allotted time period, you are entitled to a compensation that *totals* at least $75 and not more than $400.

Note: If you are bumped from a flight and, as a result, are unable to make a connecting flight, you are entitled to be compensated for both the flight from which you were bumped and the flight with which you were unable to connect.

Note: You do *not* have to take the compensation the airline offers you. If you feel it is inadequate, you may press for a larger sum by dealing with the airline or by going to court. *Note:* You do *not* have to accept alternate flights to different airports in the same metropolitan areas as your original flight.

THE EXCEPTIONS

These rules of compensation do not apply on Alaskan "bush" lines, intra-state commuter lines, charter flights and flights originating and terminating outside of the U.S.

They do not apply if boarding is denied because of government requisition of the aircraft, flight delay because of bad weather or substitution of smaller equipment on flight than originally scheduled.

You must accept seating on your ticketed flight even if it is in another class than your ticket originally specified. If you have reserved a first-class seat, you will be refunded the price difference. If you first booked a flight on coach, you do *not* have to pay for a first-class seat if that is all that is available. Airlines must offer first-class seating if coach is overbooked and first is not full.

THE PROCESS

If you get to the airport ticket counter, ticket in hand, and are denied boarding, follow these steps.

—Keep calm. Airline personnel will tune you out if you rant and rave. Calm, informed persistence is the most effective technique to use.

—Get the name of the airline employee with whom you are dealing.

—Decide if you are willing to volunteer to be bumped. If you are—arrange for compensation—if not follow these steps:

—Find out if they think they will be able to get you to your destination within two–four hours of your scheduled arrival.

—If not *and* if you need to get to your destination, have the airlines check all other scheduled flights—they have that information at their fingertips—and arrange for another airline to fly you.

—Arrange to obtain immediate compensation for your denied boarding.

—Let the airlines know you are aware of your rights and that you expect them to be observed. The meek do not inherit the seat!

THE APPEAL TO A HIGHER AUTHORITY

If the airline fails to observe the rules outlined above or if you feel that the compensation offered you is not enough, you should pursue your claim through the corporate hierarchy. If appeals to airline executives fail, then contact one of the consumer protection agencies outlined in the next chapter. The U.S. government service is The Office of the Consumer Advocate, The Civil Aeronautics Board, Washington, D.C. 20428.

DELAYED OR CANCELED FLIGHTS

Many factors can cause a flight to be delayed or canceled: bad weather, faulty equipment, airport problems, etc., are all frequent contributors to this problem. In the U.S. the airlines are required to provide their passengers with certain amenities if this happens. Often the airlines do *not* offer these services. You have to ask. Below is an outline of the air traveler's rights in such circumstances.

THE LAW

Passengers who experience delays of more than four hours must be provided with meals and communication (access to telephone or telegraph facilities) and limited ground transportation.

Hotels should be provided between the hours of 10:00 P.M. and 6:00 A.M.

Meals should be provided at any time a delayed flight would have served a meal.

THE VARIATIONS

Certain airlines' standards are different from the minimum requirements.

Allegheny provides hotel service to passengers who reside in the metropolitan area where they have been delayed if weather conditions make road conditions hazardous for drivers. Meals are not provided when the replacement flight is scheduled to serve a meal. Communication is available by a three-minute phone call or a 15-word message through the airline's own communication system.

American provides a hotel only if you are in a city where you are making a connection or in a city to which you have been rerouted.

Braniff provides the same hotel service as American. Meals are provided for delays over one hour that occur during mealtimes.

Continental provides the same hotel service as American. Meals include two free cocktails.

Delta provides a hotel only if the delay is more than four hours. Meals are provided at mealtimes. Communication is limited to a three-minute phone call.

Eastern provides the same services that Delta does.

Frontier provides a hotel after 9:00 P.M. if the delay is expected to last past midnight. During the day a hotel is provided to the ill or handicapped and to mothers with children if the delay is more than three hours. Meals are served at all mealtimes.

National allows communication if the delay is more than one hour.

Piedmont provides meals on the ground even if no meal was scheduled on the delayed flight.

TWA permits international communication through its own communications system.

United furnishes a hotel only in cities where passengers are making a connection or where the plane has been rerouted.

Western allows communication to Canada.

THE PROCESS

If you find yourself stranded in a strange airport, follow these suggestions about who to see and what to say.

—Contact airline personnel at the gate or ticket counter immediately. Find out what they know about the delay and what services they will provide.

—Ask for a chit for free food at the airport restaurant. If they give you a chit, find out what it covers. Tip? Liquor? If no chit is given, ask for information about how they work out compensations.

—Ask for a hotel if the delay occurs at night or if you have small children.

—Ask for free transportation to and from the airport and hotel. The airline should provide bus accommodations or taxi fare. If prepayment of fare or free transportation is not arranged, find out how they will compensate you.

—Ask for more than the basic law requires. The airline may be glad to provide you with a meal in situations where it is not a strict requirement. They won't volunteer it, though, so ask!

—Insist on meals during mealtimes.

—If you cannot get your baggage and need personal toiletries, ask for money to purchase them. If no prepayment is possible, make sure you get a commitment from them to repay you upon presentation of receipt.

Note: Remember, always ask the airline personnel for the accommodations that are due you *before* you go charging off. The most important thing to do is to make contact with an airline representative, get his name, and make him aware that you know what your rights are.

LOST OR DAMAGED BAGGAGE

Like the new regulations covering Free Baggage Allowance, the rules about lost and damaged bags were not meant to be understood by a person with a logical mind. The tangle of regulations and exceptions is a prime example of how the airlines set up consumer compensation programs that hurt as often as they help. Let's see why. . .

THE LOST BAGS LAW

DOMESTIC

The maximum liability per passenger is $750 (regardless of how many bags you have or the aggregate value of their contents).

INTERNATIONAL

The maximum liability is $9.07 per pound for checked bags, and $400 for carry-on luggage.

Claims filed within 45 days of loss are valid and must be evaluated by the airlines. They can no longer ignore your claim simply because you did not file it immediately. However, you will still get the best service and attention if you follow through quickly, without delay or hesitation.

THE PROCESS

DOMESTIC FLIGHTS

Even though the law does not require you to notify the airlines of your loss immediately, we advise you to do so. You will get the most attention and best service if you act promptly.

—Obtain a copy of the form "Notice of Baggage Irregularity." You can pick it up from the ticket check-in counter or the airlines baggage office (near the baggage claim area).

—Do not surrender your baggage claim check. Make a copy of it and give that to the airlines.

—Get the name of the airline personnel with whom you are dealing.

—Remember! The form you fill out at the airport is a preliminary form. A detailed claim form will be mailed to you. This is the official claim form and is due 45 days after loss.

—Filing for dollars! To substantiate your claim of loss, include sales slips and proof of ownership (insurance, etc.) whenever possible. The airlines are loath to pay you for objects they have no proof you ever owned. *Remember!* The law does *not require* you to have sales slips to claim ownership and loss of an item. Don't let the airline tell you differently.

—If you do *not* receive the official claim form within 14 days from date of loss, send a return receipt requested letter to their local office stating that they are responsible for the delay in filing for the compensation and that you want the form. Keep the receipt! The form *must be filed* within 45 days! Do not neglect this. The airline is glad to take any negligence on your part as an indication that the claim is not serious.

INTERNATIONAL FLIGHTS

Go immediately to the airline ticket counter and request a copy of the "Property Irregularity Report." The law requires that you fill this form out *immediately* upon discovery that your bags are missing. This form is only a preliminary report. The official claim form will be sent to you. You must return it completed within 21 days.

Follow all other steps as for domestic flights.

Note: Remember to keep records of all your dealings with the airline, the date, the person and the subjects discussed. The airlines do not like to pay for these losses, and you will need all the supporting evidence you can muster.

THE RUB

Even if you follow all the steps listed above, *devaluation* is taken on the items that you have lost. You will rarely get full value on any loss.

Take out *excess value insurance* on your baggage before you depart. The cost is nominal and the feeling of peace of mind is priceless.

There are countries that do not subscribe to any of the rules listed above. They are the countries that have not signed the Warsaw Convention. They are not willing to assume responsibility for cameras, money, jewelry, silverware, paintings and fragile items, etc. For example, if you fly to Turkey, where the convention rules do not apply, never fly with any of the above-listed valuables without the proper insurance.

THE DAMAGED BAGS LAW

Like the lost baggage law, the maximum liability assumed by any airline is $750 per passenger on *domestic* flights. Maximum liability assumed by the airline is $9.07 per pound plus $4 for carry-on luggage on *international* flights. *Note:* These are maximum liabilities and in no way reflect the amount you can expect to get as a settlement. Preliminary domestic claims must be filed before you leave the airport. If you take your bag off the airport grounds without making a report, you will have a hard time proving airline responsibility. Preliminary international claims must also be made immediately upon receipt of baggage.

THE PROCESS (ALL FLIGHTS)

When your bag is damaged, go to the airline ticket counter immediately and fill out a "Baggage Damage Report" form; get the name of the person you are dealing with; do *not* give up your baggage claim ticket. (Make a copy if the airline really needs one.)

Remember the form you fill out at the airport is a preliminary one. The official claim form will be sent to your home or office.

Final *domestic* claim forms for damaged baggage must be filed within 45 days. Final *international* claim forms for damaged baggage must be filed within *seven* days.
Note: For both damaged and lost baggage, the burden of proof is on you. In either case, you must prove that you have a right to be compensated for the airline's mistake. The best way to deal with such situations is to keep a level head, a detailed record and your fingers crossed. Do not hesitate. Do not let the airline stall. And when all else fails, consult

the next chapter for detailed information on who to complain to in the government and how to find proconsumer groups that will take up your cause.

OTHER PROBLEMS
OTHER SOLUTIONS

Delayed baggage is a common problem. It occurs when your bags are misrouted or delayed but are recovered within a period of hours or days. They were not lost—exactly—only sidetracked. But what happens to you if the delay of your bags for several hours or days means that you have to buy replacements of clothing or toiletries? Now, you can be reimbursed for such "inconveniences."

THE PROCESS

—Upon discovery of delayed bags, go immediately to the airline ticket counter and request money for emergency supplies. Airlines are now required to compensate you for your inconvenience up to $750.

—You will not be sure that a "delay" is not a "loss" until your bag appears sometime later. Therefore, file the "Notice of Baggage Irregularity" form at the ticket counter or baggage service office *immediately*.

—Arrange for the airline to pay you cash to replace needed items, obtain chits for use in airport shops, arrange for reimbursement at a later date upon presentation of receipts, etc. Each airline will deal with this in one or more of the methods mentioned. Get it straight before you spend your own money so that you do not make it harder to get compensation.

—If you need to buy particularly expensive items, if you lose money on vacation plans you cannot keep because you are delayed, if you lose valuable working time, or if you feel you need to be compensated for other more expensive and less tangible inconveniences, make a formal presentation of your bill, broken down into individual items. Send this to the airline ticket office where you purchased your ticket or to the executive offices.

This presentation should include: all receipts for purchases of personal items; all receipts for food purchases made while waiting for your luggage to appear; an appointment schedule that lists those meetings that you missed because of delayed baggage; copies of confirmed reservations from hotels, tours, boat, car rental or other vacation plans that you could not honor because of your delayed baggage.

APPEAL TO A HIGHER AUTHORITY

If you find that you were not treated fairly in the handling of a lost or damaged baggage claim or if you have any other complaint about the way the airline or airport you used was operated, you may consult Chapter Four for complete information on who's minding your business. The agencies listed there will offer you advice on procedures and, in some instances, will follow up your complaint with direct contact to the airline. The results can be important not only for an individual air traveler but for all airline passengers. You do the whole country a service by bringing airline transgressions to the attention of the government and private groups that seek to regulate them.

LEGAL ACTIONS

If all else fails, you can go to court to press your claims for compensation.

—Small claims court is a limited liability court that is open to all people. You do not need a lawyer to bring your case before the judge. Any case involved with $500 or less is accepted. Call your local courthouse and ask about the claim forms for this court. After you have filled out the information requested, you will be notified when the court date is set. You must appear then to explain your case.

—State and federal courts are the arenas for larger compensation claims and for suits filed against airports, airlines and the government after an airline accident. Crash victims who survive an accident may sue any of the above parties for both punitive damages and compensation.

Deceased victims' families may file only for compensation. (A California court has ruled that this distinction between crash victims and crash survivors is unfair and there may be a national precedent set by this ruling.)

Settlements can be quite large. The largest claim ever paid to an individual was $876,000. The highest claim ever paid to a family was $1,200,000.

SAFETY COMPLAINTS

Safety complaints are also important. If you feel that any airline personnel or airport employee acted in a way that threatened the safety of passengers or aircraft write to Community and Consumer Liaison Division, APA-400, Federal Aviation Administration, 800 Independence Avenue S.W., Washington, D.C. 20591.

SUMMARY

You must be assertive and attentive when dealing with the airlines. There are a set of reasonably helpful laws which, when enforced, provide you with fair recourse for any mistreatment you experience. The key to getting that fair treatment is knowledge of what the laws are.

There is little to be gained from yelling. To repeat, the airline employees will tune you out. But self-assured insistence on what you know to be fair treatment, backed by correct information, can rarely lead you astray.

Keep careful records of all your dealings with the airlines *before trouble happens;* then if something goes wrong, you can present your case with strength. Make a note of who you speak to whenever you talk to the airlines. Ask for written confirmations of all plans if time allows. Keep a record of your ticket number—separate from your ticket—and keep a cool head.

CHAPTER THREE
WHO'S RUNNING
THE SHOW?

The age of air travel began modestly as a ragtag assortment of small, irregularly operated airlines, run by swashbuckling (and not so swashbuckling) pilot/adventurers who braved the uncertainties and technical shortcomings of their aircraft at great personal risk. The magnificent men and their flying machines are almost ancient history. As in any business, growth has meant consolidation and acquisition. Many major airlines such as United and American are conglomerates or results of mergers of smaller airlines. Time flies, as they say, and today's air travel is big business.

Big business, with all its attendant benefits and problems, is here. On the plus side, there is a high level of efficiency in the transportation and processing of millions of passengers annually. Routes are direct and plentiful, and the formulation of worldwide standards for aircraft, airports and airline personnel has made flying incredibly safe. However, sheer size and the immense power inherent in any major industry has often made the airlines seem (and be) impersonal, arrogant and unresponsive to real consumer needs. Of necessity, many governmental agencies now function solely to secure the needs of the airlines and their public and to exercise control over an industry that has grown by leaps and bounds and in which safety and operating standards are of tantamount importance.

In the following section we take a look at these organizations, domestic and international, public and private. We tell you what they do and who they do it for. Are they here to serve you or to undermine you?

GOVERNMENT REGULATORY AGENCIES AND PRIVATE AIR INDUSTRY ORGANIZATIONS

DOMESTIC

DOT—*The Department of Transportation* is a cabinet level department that was formed in 1966. It is responsible for setting the general governmental policy for all areas of public transportation. The Federal Aviation Administration is a division of DOT. DOT itself has not been as forceful as it was hoped it would be when it was first formed. It does not provide much innovative leadership in areas of public concern and leaves all matters related to civil aviation to the FAA and the Civil Aeronautics Board (see below).

FAA—*The Federal Aviation Administration* is a government agency that is directed by a presidentially appointed administrator. It is a very powerful and important agency. Some of its functions are listed below.

*The FAA develops guidelines for safety of aircraft and air flight procedures. It monitors development of new technologies and watches for any problems that should be corrected.

*The FAA can initiate experimental and developmental projects. This is a very special authorization. It allows the government to become a partner with the industry and to request and follow through on special innovative ideas.

*The FAA controls the rights to all U.S. airspace. This means that it can define what airspace may be used by the military, commercial and private aircraft. It is *not* responsible for the routes of individual airlines. (See CAB below.)

*The FAA runs Dulles Airport in Washington, D.C.

*The FAA certifies the structural soundness of all new aircraft designs and prototypes before they go into production.

*The FAA sets the standards for pilot licensing.

CAB—*The Civil Aeronautics Board* is the single most important government agency that deals with commercial air travel. The CAB was set up in 1938. It has enormous powers to oversee and regulate all nonmilitary air travel. Some of its functions are listed below:

*The CAB regulates competition between the airlines in the U.S. This is the most important and most controversial power it has, because by determining what routes the various airlines may fly and by setting the fares they may charge, the CAB is directly responsible for where you fly, how you fly, and what you pay for the "privilege." The CAB is trying to step out of this role somewhat by instituting "Deregulation."

Deregulation is a broad term used to describe a change in the rules governing the CAB's authority to set fares and assign routes to U.S. airlines. The traditional role of the CAB as final arbiter of all aspects of competition (by controlling when, where, and at what price the airlines could fly) is now being completely changed. The airlines will be free to enter markets as they choose. Fares will be free to "float" to whatever the market will bear. Some residual control—for the public good—will be retained by the CAB. The CAB will be concerned primarily with safety standards, fair and open competition, and maintenance of good service to all parts of the U.S., including small and often unprofitable towns and cities.

Logically, all this appears to be for the good of the consumer—more competition, lower prices, more choices. But, unfortunately, nothing is ever completely logical. The CAB, which initiated the drive toward "deregulation," was forced at one point to testify *against* the law as Congress was writing it. They said "the most fundamental concern we (the CAB) have involves the rate provisions which . . . on its surface appears to provide fare flexibility. However, as a practical matter, price moderating disciplines of competition (will not) operate in many markets." In other words, in the new law there is a chance that prices could actually rise in some areas instead of fall! Done fairly, deregulation could prove a real boon to the U.S. consumer, but vigilant attention to the legislative process is needed to make sure that deregulation is not a wild free-for-all that sacrifices the consumer's best interests.

NTSB—*The National Transportation Safety Board* is an independent federal agency that oversees the safety of all types of public and private transportation in this country. Below is a list of its functions:

*The NTSB sets up laws governing the procedures for reporting aircraft accidents. All investigations are conducted by the NTSB itself. Their purpose is to determine the cause of an accident.

*The NTSB recommends new safety standards and modifications in aircraft structure or procedure as a result of its accident investigation findings.

The NTSB issues a series of pamphlets listing all air crashes in a year and the statistics, information and cause. The incidents are broken down into categories: Weather as a Cause, Turbine Powered Aircraft, Missing or Missing and Later Recovered Aircraft, Alcohol as a Cause, Air Taxi Operations, and others. If you are interested in receiving any of these or if you have any specific questions about air safety write to Publication Branch, National Transportation Safety Board, Washington, D.C. 20594.

ATA—*The Air Transport Association of America* is a private nongovernmental organization, with a membership made up of 24 U.S. commercial airlines. By sharing information among themselves, the airlines can learn new procedures and make safety suggestions that will benefit all companies and passengers. This is the most important function of this organization. Its other purposes are less well defined but probably of more far-reaching consequence. ATA is a strong business organization that applies pressure on government officials and agencies to protect its interests. It acts as a subtle instrument for industry-wide cooperation on matters of pricing and services. It is the local model of the IATA (see below under International). For information you may contact ATA at 1709 New York Avenue, N.W., Washington, D.C. 20006.

INTERNATIONAL

IATA—*The International Air Transport Association* is an immensely powerful international organization made up of most of the world's commercial airlines. But deregulation of U.S. airlines has severely undermined its authority—much to the dismay of its non-American membership. U.S. airlines, now free from government regulation of fares, are insisting on freedom from IATA's traditional price-fixing regulations. For information about what IATA does, see the list below:

*IATA once set standards for air fares for all its member airlines. No member airline could undercut the price agreed on by all airlines. All major airlines used to charge the same fares. This is changing. Even budget and standby fares are the same for each IATA airline.

*IATA does provide certain important services to the member airlines *and* the flying public. They could maintain these functions and give up their price-fixing activities and still be a useful organization.

—All technical information discovered worldwide is shared among the members. This allows even small countries to benefit from expensive technical discoveries.

—Currency exchanges are handled through an IATA clearinghouse. All payments by airlines must be made in local currency wherever they fly. To simplify this complicated financial system, IATA provides computer-banking services and assistance.

—International standards of conduct, procedures and methods are enforced. This assures an airline that its pilots can land anywhere by using the same system.

—Safety standards are enforced and improvements are made whenever needed. (Theoretically, at least.)
Note: There are some very fine international airlines that do not subscribe to IATA. They are well run, safe, modern airlines. All the information they need is available to them. They handle their business affairs in other ways.

ICAO—*The International Civil Aviation Organization* is an association of more than 135 different governments or governmental agencies that cooperatively set international standards and laws for aviation. ICAO sees to it that all technical information about developments in aviation is available to its members. Without such an organization, there would be no standardization of equipment or methods, and planes and personnel would not all meet the same high standards. This organization functions as IATA claims to do. It is different, however, in that the individual companies are not directly represented.

CHAPTER FOUR
WHO'S MINDING
YOUR BUSINESS?

Luckily, a surprising number of organizations are minding your business. These much-needed groups are the watchdogs of the industry, the voices for change, the pursuers of industry misdeeds. They are here to help you *and* they need your help. You can call on any of these consumer-oriented organizations if you have a question about what you should do, how you should proceed, and who you should see about a complaint when troubles arise.

In some instances the organizations will pursue the complaint for you if you have tried unsuccessfully to resolve it yourself. Others will make recommendations to the government for changes in the general regulations that govern the industry, thereby helping to prevent the recurrence of the problem you have had. They cannot assist you directly, however. Certain groups are concerned with safety, others with service, some with comfort, some with prices, but all of them depend on your support financially, morally or through your active support of consumer plans being considered in Congress.

OCA—*The Office of the Consumer Advocate* is part of the Civil Aeronautics Board. The OCA-CAB is the most important governmental lobby for air travelers. Because of the

OCA's position within the CAB, it is constantly making recommendations to Congress about legislation, and it has clout whenever it deals with the airlines, whether it is in making sweeping recommendations or pursuing your individual complaint.

*To enlist the help of the OCA in pursuing a complaint against an airline for failure to offer just compensation for misdeeds or any other transgressions, follow these steps.

—Follow all avenues open to you before you call on the OCA. Call all the local managers, and write to the executives at the airline headquarters. If that fails turn to the OCA.

—Write a simple letter stating in detail what happened (or failed to happen) to you and all the steps you have taken on your own to get compensation from the airline.

—Make sure you include all information about your flight—its date, time and airline and, if possible, your ticket number and the names of those employees at the airline that you have spoken to.

*The OCA will respond as soon as possible. They will inform you of what additional steps you may take, what they can do and what cannot be done. For assistance write Office of the Consumer Advocate, Civil Aeronautics Board, Washington, D.C. 20428.

ACAP—*The Aviation Consumer Action Project,* a Ralph Nader organization, is an important consumer action group. Of all the organizations that exist to serve the public, it is the only one that is free of both governmental affiliation and commercial motivations. Since this group has no secondary affiliation, it has no need to mince its words or to curb its activities. It is an outspoken project, often present at congressional hearings on aviation legislation and a frequent lobby for new protective consumer-oriented laws. Because this is an independent organization, it does not always have the time or the money to pursue individual complaints. They are glad to hear about the problems you have, however, because it helps them become aware of areas that need their attention. They will also send you some basic advice sheets and answer specific questions that you may ask. They depend on consumer contributions for much of their funding, so . . .

For information on the organization, a copy of their fact sheet on air rights or advice, write The Aviation Consumer Action Project, P.O. Box 19029, Washington, D.C. 20036.

APA—*The Airline Passengers Association* exists for two, hopefully not contradictory, purposes. First, they are a traveler's insurance group, offering extensive coverage for all forms of travel—from trolley to turbojet. Lloyd's of London is the underwriter, and the rates and variety of coverage are extensive, if you are interested in that sort of thing. Second, they provide consumers with advice and warnings on bad travel arrangements and go to Washington to testify on legislative measures that are of interest to travelers. Their annual survey of membership is highly regarded, and they use it as a basis for formulation of their consumer advocate role. For a complete look at their latest survey, see chapter six.

*Membership entitles you to their *Holiday* magazine, their regular newsletters and insurance. You may join and get *no* insurance solicitations if you so request.

*For information on membership fees and benefits, write to Airline Passengers Association, P.O. Box 2758, Dallas, Texas 75221.

APA—*The Air Line Pilots Association* is an AFL-CIO affiliated union, representing 32,000 pilots and 15,000 flight attendants. It serves not only its membership's labor-related needs, but helps the entire airline industry by providing a forum for exchange of information, suggested improvements, and personnel needs between the workers and the managers of the airlines and airports in the U.S. The reason it is included in this survey of consumer-oriented groups is that it is responsible for the publication of an annual review of the world's worst airports. See chapter seven for a look at this year's list. For more information write Air Line Pilots Association, 1625 Massachusetts Avenue, N.W., Washington, D.C. 20036.

ASTA—*The American Society of Travel Agents*, Office of Consumer Affairs, is part of this huge professional organization. It exists to monitor ASTA's membership and to deal with complaints brought against airlines, tour operators or any other organizations that sell travel services. Anyone who wishes to make a complaint against a member travel agent should contact this office. A special service is provided to persons who have *not yet purchased* their travel plans. If you are considering buying a tour, for example, you may call any ASTA office and find out if it has any record of unsettled complaints against the company. ASTA will not recommend any service but it will give you this valuable information if it can. If you have any question about how you were treated by your travel agent or any complaints about the services you purchased, write: ASTA, Office of Consumer Affairs, 711 Fifth Avenue, New York, New York 10022.

FSF—*The Flight Safety Foundation* is one of those organizations you rarely hear about—but you should be very glad it's there. This highly technical nonprofit organization is sponsored by many large travel-related companies. FSF publishes many high-quality publications on such topics as safe fueling, aircraft safety, improvement suggestions, and more. Their monthly newsletter, sent to all members, contains current information on business trends and technical innovations, plus newsy information on industry personalities. They are highly respected and often discover urgently needed improvements and make them known to industry management and workers. There is, for example, an anonymous forum for employees who feel certain dangerous conditions exist in their aircraft or hangars but who are afraid to "go public" because they might lose their jobs or be ostracized by their fellow workers for being outspoken. For detailed information about the services and publications of this important organization, write the Flight Safety Foundation, 1800 North Kent Road, Arlington, Virginia 22209.

SUMMARY

Find out what regulations govern your air journey. They change frequently; they are often complex. It does take some work on your part. You must ask questions constantly. Why is this? What's the rule? Who do I talk to? You must pay attention to information in the papers. And you must write to your airline, your legislator and your consumer advocate when you feel strongly about an issue such as deregulation, or denied-boarding compensation.

Perhaps someday the air industry, such an important part of our modern lives, will become a partner with the consumer not an adversary. Until that day—*beware* and *be wary. The seat you save may be your own!*

CHAPTER FIVE
FARE PLAY
(A TRAGICOMEDY)

The unfair fare farce is the most difficult obstacle any traveler has to overcome in order to have a good vacation. You may think that it is hard to get the right change from a street vendor in the Casbah! Just try and get the right fare for your needs from your airline!

Now, it isn't that the airlines are out to cheat you. It is just that the tangle of fares has become so complicated that even the airlines' employees have trouble unraveling the information. There are regular fares, discount fares, promotional fares, excursion fares, charter fares, package fares, temporary fares and more. It is enough to reduce the heartiest of travellers to tears. This has happened because the last several years have seen sweeping changes in the structure of the airline industry in the U.S.

Deregulation, which began as a tentative venture allowing some loosening of regulations governing routes and fares, has exploded into a full scale free-for-all. Once fares were uniform—if American gave you a discount, you could be sure all competing airlines would match that discount penny for penny. That is not true any longer. The CAB has decided that any airline may reduce coach fares up to 70 percent off prevailing rates and may sell first-class tickets at whatever the market will bear.

This means that you may find that one airline has a short-time, loss-leading fare—just like your local super-market—while another is still charging you the same old pre-deregulation price. Braniff went so far as to offer a four-day standby excursion from Dallas-Fort Worth to Las Vegas for $7 coach class, $11 first-class!

Luckily, all *is not* pandemonium—there are certain industry-wide trends—ones that you can learn about and look for. They are as follows:

Budget flights—Tickets sold on these flights are purchased 21 days before the *week* you want to fly. The airline tells you the day and time you will fly, one to two weeks before your departure. Then you have a reservation.

(Sample prices: New York to London—$169, London to New York—$130. These fares represent a savings of 61 percent over regular coach fares.)

Standby flights—This rebirth of the old '60's student standby type fare is now available to everyone—on certain routes and in limited numbers. It generally costs the same as its companion budget fare, but tickets are sold three hours prior to the flight and have no cancellation penalty attached.

APEX or advanced purchase excursion fares—These are available to most destinations for travelers who can prepay 45–21 days in advance. (An APEX fare is a prepayment air-only reservation that offers Europe-bound travelers a low-cost round-trip flight.)

Package, charter, and prepaid promotional fares—These are available in many situations. A detailed explanation follows in this chapter. Such fares offer 30–50 percent discounts (or more!) when purchased three to eight weeks early. (The one-price-unlimited mileage-set-time fare now offered by most U.S. airlines lets you jet around the country—making unlimited stops, going as far as you want, for one price!)

NEW DEVELOPMENTS

Deregulation has brought with it certain very new and interesting trends. Among them are:

The authorization for supplemental airlines (that is, unscheduled and charter airline companies), such as World Airlines, to fly regular flights within the U.S. World has a $99 special from New York to Los Angeles, cutting the traditional discount fares by 50 percent!

The freedom of airlines to enter and leave markets pretty much as they choose. This means an airline can fly where it wants, when it wants—for any price it wants. This will certainly cause some routes—now "under used"—to be dropped, resulting in curtailed service to smaller population centers.

Three classes of service are emerging: *First*—with its traditional luxuries and then some, *Second*—for business and last-minute travelers who pay full coach fare, and *Third*—for the great jumble of budget, standby, excursion and charter passengers who give up hot meals, legroom and movies for low prices.

Airline mergers—especially between small and middle-sized lines (or absorption by larger lines)—seem inevitable as increased competition, lower fares and the need for greater passenger loads to keep profits high, threaten to sink those companies without the capital or the resources and planes to fight the battle.

Look for the entry of foreign airlines into the national market sometime in the future. Exactly how this will be done is still up in the air but, whatever the plan, it should keep the airways jumpin'!

TRAVEL TIPS

The fare structure of domestic and international airlines is changing almost daily—and will continue to do so for the next couple of years as the industry responds and reacts to the effects of deregulation. Eventually, things should stabilize, the fares re-order, and the competition diminish, as the victors consolidate their position.

But for now you have to deal with the amazing mess of new information and regulations. The best way to handle this mishmash is to follow the pointers below:

Call more than one airline. Unlike the old days, it is possible to get a lower fare from one line than from another. So if you are flying to Los Angeles, call Western, American, TWA, etc., and let them make you an offer you can't refuse.

Keep asking "Are there any other fare plans?"

Read all the available travel literature yourself. Do not give up all responsibility for making arrangements. If you are well informed, you can get the best service from those with whom you deal.

Get the fare summary that each airline is required to provide to all prospective passengers on request. It will give you a concise outline of some of the fares offered. (For a complete list you will have to write to the address listed in the summary.) Ask for all literature available on promotional fares. These fares are special short-term offerings that provide dramatic savings to passengers flying to specific locations.

Book your flight early. Many of the major discounts are available to those who prepay their flights. These fares often require that flights be booked up to 60 days before departure.

When booking any land arrangements with or without an air fare package, ask yourself these questions: How far is the hotel from city center or beach? Are the prices of meals reasonable? Are meals a fixed menu or a la carte? What are the local sight-seeing attractions? Does the tour include the ones I am interested in? What national holidays occur while I am abroad? Will they interfere with sight-seeing plans?

What expenses are *not* covered? Extra meals? Land transportation? Tour fees? Tips? Airport taxes?

Be as flexible as possible. Many discount fares have minimum and maximum length of visit requirements. If you can arrange your schedule so that you can take advantage of these lower fares, do so.

Read all contracts for hotels, tours or charters very carefully. The clauses that cover cancellation penalties, airline and tour responsibilities to you and the ability of the tour operator to substitute alternative lodging or plans if "needed," are all very important. Don't sign what you don't understand.

Always buy cancellation insurance to protect yourself from having to pay a penalty if you are unable to take the flight that you paid for ahead of time. This insurance should be purchased when you make your reservation.

If you fly with children, be aware that the overall cost is not always lowest if you choose the lowest *adult* fare available. This is the case because children's fares often increase as adults' are lowered.

Take a deep breath. Read on! You've nothing to fear but fares themselves!

THE PLOT OUTLINE

Below is an outline of the fare play: what is available, what the conditions and restrictions of each fare are and who offers the best fares.

There are many types of fares. To give you an idea of the variety now available, here is a list of United's domestic fares and TWA's international fares. These are by no means complete or final. New fares come and go all the time. But this will give you a rough idea of the variety and confusion!

UNITED'S DOMESTIC FARES

First-Class	Super Saver
Deluxe Night	Adult, child, peak,
Coach	shoulder, and off-peak
Coach Night	rate for each fare
Economy	Individual Ski Tour
Economy Night	Fares
Senior Citizen	Freedom Fares (one
Commuter Standby	price ticket—unlimited
Weekend Excursion	mileage)
Midweek Fares	Group Inclusive Tour
Florida Midweek Fares	Peak, off-peak and week-
21-Day Midweek Fares	end rates
Excursions—	Advanced Purchase Ex-
Coach	cursion APEX

United's Individual Tour Basing

7-day Coach
14-day Coach
21-day Coach

Group Travel

16-day excursion
30-day with land arrangements

TWA's INTERNATIONAL FARES

First
Coach
Excursion
   14-21 day
   22-45 day
   14-45 day Advanced Purchase
   Excursion APEX
No reservation Standby

Budget
Midweek 56% discount
Youth
7-8 Group Inclusive Tour
14-21 Group Inclusive
   Tour
Affinity groups (for travel
   clubs)

What follows is a survey of the basic fare structures common to all U.S. domestic and international airlines.

DOMESTIC FARES

FIRST-CLASS

This VIP fare offers the benefits of faster check-in, more spacious seating, fancier menus, more attentive in-flight service, free liquor and speedy baggage delivery upon arrival.

Seasons—None. This fare is constant all year round.

Validity—A first-class ticket is good for up to one year after purchase.

Purchase—No advanced purchase necessary.

COACH CLASS

This is the standard air fare. All discounts are measured against this fare. The coach class occupies most of the plane, and persons who buy cheaper fares are seated with those who pay full fares. A new special service to full-fare passengers is being offered. It provides for a limited number of coach seats in the front of the cabin to be set aside (and partitioned or curtained off) for those who pay full rates. It offers a child-free, quieter ride with more in-flight services, a special check-in counter and faster baggage delivery at your point of arrival. You must request this service when you make your reservation because the number of seats is limited.

Seasons—None. This fare is constant all year round.

Validity—A coach ticket is good for up to one year from date of purchase.

Purchase—No advanced purchase necessary.

CHILDREN'S FARE

Each adult fare has a separate child's fare that goes with it. The child's fare is two-thirds of the price of the adult fare. In other words, if a coach passenger pays $300 for his ticket, his child traveling with him will pay $200.

Restrictions—This fare applies to children traveling with an adult and who are between the ages of 2 and 12.

INFANT'S FARE

Each adult fare has a separate infant's fare that goes with it. The infant's fare for full-fare adults traveling with a child is *free*—if the child does not occupy a seat.

SENIOR CITIZENS FARE

Discounts for seniors are now available.

Purchase—Reservations can be made up to 24 hours before the flight. Payment must be made at least one hour before the flight.

Discounts—Prices are up to 50 percent off regular coach fares.

NIGHT FARES

This fare applies to certain flights, nationwide, that have limited seats set aside for reduced fare passengers between the hours of 9:00 or 10:00 P.M. and 6:00 A.M. The savings is generally 20 percent over the standard coach fare. (You may travel first-class on night coach for the price of a regular day-coach ticket.)

Seasons—None. This fare is constant all year round.

Validity—A night coach is valid up to one year after purchase on any flight with night coach seats.

Purchase—No advanced purchase necessary.

Restrictions–No general restrictions. May be made available or not at the discretion of the airline.

Coach Class Night—The cost is 20 percent less than day coach.

Children's Night Coach—The cost is 33⅓ percent off adult night coach fare.

LEISURE CLASS

This special fare, available on Eastern, offers the possibility of a free flight. No wonder you haven't heard much about it!

The steps to take to qualify follow:

Purchase ticket at full coach price but have it designated leisure class. You will not have a confirmed reservation.

If after all regular passengers are seated on your flight, the airline cannot find room for you, they must give you an *immediate refund*.

You fly free on the next available flight to your destination.

This fare is particularly useful if you are not in a big hurry but you really want to get somewhere immediately and most flights are booked full. You can count on the fact that the airline does *not* want to give you a free ride. Even with overbooking, you are a likely candidate for a seat. If you *don't* get on, you win and if you *do* get on, you win. It is not often that the airlines will let the traveler in on such a good deal!

EXCURSION FARES

These fares are designed for vacationers who are traveling for a defined period of time. Each excursion fare has a minimum and maximum stay restriction. For example, if a traveler is going to be away for 16 days, a 14–21 day excursion fare will apply. These fares come in many forms. Below are the main domestic plans. (In addition to the standard type of excursions listed below, there are short-term, midweek, weekend and off-season fares that offer great savings to specific locations.)

7–30-DAY EXCURSION FARE

This is a 7-day minimum/30-day maximum stay plan. It offers 20–25 percent savings over regular coach fares. This is the standard domestic excursion plan.

Seasons—Yes. Travelers will be charged slightly different rates at different times of the year. The seasons are determined by the heaviest or "peak" periods of travel.

Peak—The most expensive time of the year is generally from June 1 to September 14.

Off—This is the slow time of the year, and the air rates are lower to encourage more people to fly. "Off" rates are in effect from mid-September to May 31.

Exceptions—Resort areas in this country such as Florida have different seasons. Peak—High fares are in effect from December 19 to April 30. Off—Lower rates are in effect from May 1 to December 18.

Validity—This ticket is good for the specific time period indicated. Date of departure is set at time of purchase.

Restrictions—The stipulations that define the excursion are related to each specific excursion.

CHILDREN'S FARE

Children may fly with an accompanying adult who has an excursion ticket for 50 percent of that adult fare. This is an example of the danger of paying a lower adult fare and a higher child's fare. Make sure you are saving money on your *total* bill.

TWO CLASSES OF 7–30-DAY EXCURSIONS

Day Coach Excursion—This coach class provides you with full coach facilities during daylight hours for a reduced fare.

The savings offered by this stay-restricted plan is 20 percent over regular coach.

Night Coach Excursion—This coach class provides you with full coach facilities during the hours of 9:00 P.M.-6:00 A.M. The savings offered by this stay-restricted night plan is 25 percent over regular coach.

WEEKEND EXCURSION FARES

These fares are offered in specific areas—usually resort locales—to travelers who need to fly between Friday night and Monday noon. If you are making a short jaunt to any resort or large metropolitan area, ask about the availability of this plan.

Validity—Ticket is good for specific times defined by plan.

Purchase—Ticket may be bought anytime before the flight. You must purchase a round-trip.

Restrictions—Tickets may be used from city of departure only between the hours of 7:00 P.M. Friday to 12:00 midnight Sunday and from your point of return only from midnight Friday to 12:00 noon Monday of the same weekend.

SUPER SAVER

This category of advanced payment, round-trip air fare is offered by many airlines under this—or other—names. Savings range from 30–50 percent off regular coach fares.

Seasons—Rates reflect seasonal fluctuations.

Purchase—30 days prior to departure the round-trip ticket must be reserved and paid for.

Restrictions—Minimum stay is seven days. Maximum stay is 45 days. No stopovers are permitted. Monday through Thursday are off-peak (cheaper) than Friday through Sunday, which are peak (more expensive) days to fly using this fare.

CHILDREN'S FARE

A 50 percent discount off full adult coach fare is what's offered. Here again, check your figures. One adult super saver and one child's 50 percent coach fare may add up to more money than it would if the adult paid a slightly higher fare and the child was given a greater discount.

ABC—ADVANCED BOOKING CHARTERS

This is a cheap and easy way for a vacationer to take advantage of the new discount prices without having to buy a "land package."

Seasons—Prices of air fares to change throughout the year, reflecting higher or peak rates in summer months.

Validity—Ticket is good for specific dates for which it was purchased.

Purchase—North American ABCs must be purchased 30 days before the scheduled date of departure. Replacements for cancellations are allowed for up to 15 percent of available seats. Therefore it is sometimes possible to buy an ABC ticket very near the date of departure!

Savings—An ABC offers savings of 30–50 percent over regular coach fares.

DOMESTIC DISCOUNT FARES WITH LAND PURCHASE REQUIREMENTS

The following fares are special "package" air fares that are designed to offer vacationing travelers a reduced rate on air fare and prepaid hotel, sight-seeing and tourist services. The discounted fares may not be purchased without purchase of the "land arrangements." The amount of land arrangements that must be prepurchased depends on the length of your stay and the location of the stay.

The exact provisions of each such fare plan vary widely. We have set down the basic structures of each fare. You should always check with your travel agent or airline for specific details or changes in the plans.

ITX—INDIVIDUAL TOUR BASING FARE

This fare does not require that you fly or travel with a group or that you stay in specific locations. You may arrange the trip as you want. The only requirements are that you must buy minimum amounts of land arrangements (usually a minimum of two nights' lodging and $25–$65 in food and activities).

Seasons—Seasonal adjustments in fares and in land arrangements are made.

Validity—Round-trip tickets can be used for specific tours. The most standard tour is a 7–30-day plan, but 4–30-, 7–8- and 2–3-day plans also exist. Inquire at your travel agent or airline office for specific information.

Purchase—Tickets may be purchased anytime before the flight. You must buy a round-trip ticket.

Land Purchase Requirements—These amounts vary, depending on the length and location of your stay. For short stays the minimum amount is from $25–$65 for the first several days. Longer stays have additional per diem charges. The amounts required are always less than you would spend if *you* were booking the land arrangements.

Savings—Certain west coast locales offer air fare reductions of up to 30 percent on a weekday and 20 percent on weekends over regular coach. Other locales offer 15–20 percent reductions.

CHILDREN'S FARE

In some circumstances children are allowed to fly with an adult paying an ITX fare for 50 percent less than the adult ticket. Sometimes, however, no discount is given. Add the totals here. The *total* cost of adult and child's ticket may not be a savings.

GIT—GROUP INCLUSIVE TOUR FARES

This fare is a real bargain! It offers a large air fare discount for those persons who are willing to travel with a group throughout the entire trip. The composition of the group and the size are determined by your travel agent or tour operator.

Seasons—None. The time of departure and return is determined by the ticket agent, and the price is set for the specific tour. Prices will reflect higher seasonal rates in some locales.

Validity—Ticket applies to specific dates of departure and return with group. There are several plans available. 7-8-day minimum/maximum stay and 3–14-day minimum/maximum stay plans are common.

Purchase—A reservation should be made for these tours early. Purchase is required 30 days before scheduled departure in most cases. A deposit of 10 percent of ticket price is required when you make your reservation. The deposit is *nonrefundable* if you cancel your plans at a later date.

Land Purchase Requirements—Depending on the length and location of your stay, the requirements can vary. The general requirement is $100 minimum.

Savings—The air fare on a GIT flight is about 40 percent less than the comparable regular coach fare. A tremendous buy!

OTC—ONE-STOP TOUR CHARTER

This fare offers a tremendous saving. Despite its name, it is possible to arrange for three or more stopovers between your point of departure and your point of arrival (the farthest point you travel to). The only requirement is that you *begin* and *end* your trip at the same airport.

Seasons—None. The time of departure and return is determined by the tour, and the prices are set for individual trips.

Validity—The ticket requirements vary. Generally you have to stay at least four days and three nights. Maximum stay varies.

Purchase—No advanced purchase is required. You must buy this plan from a travel agent or tour operator. Airlines cannot sell charter tours.

Land purchase—$15.00 per night/per adult. $7.50 per night/per child—2–11 years.

Savings—Enormous! The total bill for land accommodations plus air fare is often less than the price of regular coach fare alone.

Note: This particular type of charter offers savings. However, OTC tour operators *may cancel* the tour if not enough people sign up for it. There have been problems with this.

You are in *no* danger of losing your money because your fare is kept in an escrow account until after the tour is completed. What can happen is that the cancellation comes so late that you do not have time to make new plans, you do not have the money to change to a full fare coach plan or there are no available flights. So beware. This is a risky business. Non-land discount fares offer comparable savings with minimum risk. See the ABC information in this section.

Note: When buying this plan always purchase cancellation insurance that will protect *you* if the tour company cancels. This insurance is different from the cancellation insurance offered to protect travelers from default if *they* are unable to use their charter plans. This insurance, which provides you with monetary compensation for the difference in price between your initial charter fare and the more expensive replacement you must buy, can be purchased through any travel agent.

SUMMARY

The moral of this fare play is that a curious traveler can get a good deal. Ask questions about fares, accommodations and all restrictions that exist. Don't fall for a fast-talking charter salesman or be victimized by a travel agent who is reluctant to sell you a charter because of decreased commission. Insist that you be given all the information you need, to make a wise decision about your travel plans.

INTERNATIONAL FARES

FIRST-CLASS

This VIP fare offers the benefits of faster check-in, more spacious seating, fancier menus, free liquor, more attentive in-flight service, and speedy baggage delivery upon arrival.

Seasons—None. The fare is constant all year round.

Validity—A first-class ticket is good for up to one year after purchase.

Purchase—No advanced purchase requirement.

COACH CLASS

This is the standard international air fare. All discounts are measured against this fare. The coach class occupies most of the plane and persons who buy cheaper fares are seated with those who fly coach. For information on a special Full Fare Coach Service Plan that is offered on many intercontinental jumbo jets, see the Coach Class entry under Domestic Fares in this chapter.

Seasons—Yes. On international flights coach fares are subject to seasonal changes in ticket prices. The busiest time of the year is ''peak'' time and the months on either side of this time period are designated ''shoulder.'' The slowest time of the year—the cheapest—is called ''off'' season.

Peak—On international *eastbound* flights the highest fares are June, July and August. On international *westbound* flights the highest fares are July, August and September.

Shoulder—On international *eastbound* flights the months of April and May and September and October are less expensive than ''peak'' periods. On international *westbound* flights the months of April and May and June and October are less expensive than ''peak'' periods.

Off—On international *eastbound* flights the months of November through March are the least expensive. Westbound flights are reduced to ''off'' rates during the same months.

Validity—This ticket is good for up to one year after purchase.

Purchase—Ticket may be bought at any time. No advanced purchase necessary.

CHILDREN'S FARE

Children from the ages of two to twelve when traveling with an adult paying full coach fare are charged 50 percent of the adult ticket price.

INFANT'S FARE

Children under the age of two are carried on some routes for free. Certain localities require that 10 percent of adult fare be paid. No free luggage allowance is provided unless child pays at least 10 percent of adult fare.

EXCURSION FARES

International Excursion Fares offer Air-Only and Air-and-Land packages that allow a traveler to make a round-trip flight for a specific length of time at great savings. They all require advanced payments of some kind and have cancellation penalties.

14–21-DAY EXCURSIONS

These fares offer savings to travelers who plan to travel for at least 14 days and not more than 21 days.

Seasons—Yes. The prices of the excursions reflect the changes in seasons as defined under the Coach Class entry in this section of the chapter.

Validity—Ticket is bought for specific time period.

Purchase—You may buy this fare at any time before departure.

Restrictions—There are several conditions.

Stopovers—Four are permitted.

Fare availability—This plan is for flights to Europe, the Middle East and Israel.

Weekend surcharge is levied. If you fly *eastbound* on Friday or Saturday, you will have to pay an additional $15. If you fly *westbound* on Saturday or Sunday, you must pay an additional $15.

Savings—The fare is about 17 percent less than regular coach.

CHILDREN'S FARE

Children traveling with an adult who paid the excursion fare are charged 50 percent of that discount fare.

Note: This kind of excursion does not normally provide land arrangements. You can have your travel agent or tour operator set up a land/air package however. The minimum land purchase required then would be around $120 for an inclusive 14–21-day journey.

22–45-DAY EXCURSIONS

These fares are available to travelers who qualify for the minimum/maximum stay restrictions. The savings are even greater than the 14–21-day plans.

Seasons—The prices of the excursions reflect the changes in seasons as defined under the Coach Class entry in this section of the chapter.

Validity—Return segments of the ticket are good for no more than 45 days after departure. The tickets are for specified dates.

Purchase—This ticket can be purchased anytime before the departure of the flight. No advanced purchase required.

Restrictions—There are several conditions.

Stopovers—None are allowed on flights to Europe. Israel-bound flights are permitted one stop.

Middle Eastern flights are permitted three stopovers.

Fare availability—This plan is for flights to Europe, Israel and the Middle East only.

Weekend surcharge is levied.

Savings—The fare is about 23 percent less than regular coach.

CHILDREN'S FARE

Children traveling with an adult who pays the excursion fare are charged 50 percent of that discount fare.

Note: Open-Jaw booking is available on both of these excursion plans. Open-Jaw means that you may return home from a different airport than the one at which you arrived. For example, if you are traveling in Europe, you may fly from New York to Frankfurt, travel widely and wind up in Paris, from where you may then catch a flight back to New York. It is not necessary to return to Frankfurt before you depart. It is not absolutely necessary to arrange this when you buy your ticket. However, if you are traveling at peak season you may have trouble getting on a flight on which you have not obtained an early reservation. So, whenever possible, set this up ahead of time. But if impulse overtakes you while abroad, you can at least try to change your plans. Remember! Open-Jaw works only if your point of departure does not cost more than the original ticket. You aren't going to get to fly from Athens to New York if you only paid for a London–New York flight.

APEX—ADVANCED PURCHASE EXCURSION

This fare is one of the most innovative of all air fares. By planning your trip well ahead of time and paying for your flight early, you can realize unbelievable savings.

Seasons—Ticket prices do reflect the rise and fall of demand from season to season. For a complete explanation of seasons, see the Coach Class entry in the international section of the chapter.

Validity—Tickets are always sold as round trips. The law requires that the minimum stay be at least seven days. Maximum stay varies from 45–60 days. Fourteen–45 is the standard stay requirement. Ticket is valid for designated flight period only.

Purchase—Tickets to European destinations must be *paid* for 21–45 days before the scheduled departure of the flight, depending on your destination. If you are unable to make your flight, you will be penalized $50.

Restrictions—There are several conditions imposed on this fare.

Stopovers—None.

Fare application—Europe, Egypt and Israel.

Weekend surcharge is levied.

Savings—46 percent over regular coach.

CHILDREN'S FARE

Children traveling with an adult flying on an APEX fare are charged 66 percent of the adult APEX fare, or 50 percent of an applicable excursion fare—whichever is less.

HOLIDAY OR SUPER APEX

This additional APEX offers even greater savings to those who can purchase their tickets even earlier!

Seasons—Ticket prices do reflect the rise and fall of seasonal demand. For a complete explanation of seasons, see the Coach Class entry in this section of the chapter.

Validity—Tickets are sold as round trips. Minimum stay is at least 7 days, usually 14 days; maximum stay is up to 60 days, usually 45 days—depending on your destination.

Purchase—Tickets must be purchased at least 45 days in advance—except 30 days for Switzerland and 21 days for England.

Restrictions—As with all discount fares, there are several conditions imposed on the traveler.

Stopovers—None.

Fare application—England, Germany, Switzerland.

Weekend surcharge—None.

CHILDREN'S FARE

To/from Germany there is no children's discount. (Infants travel free.) To/from Switzerland 66 percent of APEX fare or 50 percent of applicable excursion fare, whichever is less. Savings—52 percent over regular coach fare.

Note: Open-Jaw is permitted with this fare. See page 92 for a complete rundown of how to use this flexible routing plan.

YOUTH FARES

This fare plan is for people from the ages of 12–21 (although some European plans allow a maximum age of 25). Its savings is of benefit to any young person who is flying on short notice. There are now plans available that offer young vacationers much higher savings.

Seasons—Yes. The seasonal changes in demand and in rates is reflected in the youth fare.

Validity—Ticket is good for up to one year after purchase.

Purchase—Ticket may be bought five or fewer days before the scheduled departure of the flight.

Restrictions—Fare applies only to flights to Europe, Israel or the Middle East.

Stopovers—None in Europe. One elsewhere.
Weekend surcharge is not levied.
Savings—This fare is 33 percent less than coach.
Note: Intra-European airlines have special fares for students and youth. If you need to fly within one country or inside Europe, check with the national airline in that area for special rates.

INTERNATIONAL FARES WITH LAND PURCHASE REQUIREMENTS

GIT—GROUP INCLUSIVE TOURS

This fare package offers tremendous savings over the regular coach fare. You must purchase and prepay for a certain amount of "land arrangements." The advantage to this sort of plan is that you are free to buy those accommodations as a member of a group or as an independent traveler.

7–8-DAY GIT

This plan requires you to stay abroad at least seven days but not more than eight. (There are exceptions—as explained below.)

Seasons—Price is determined by cost of total package and will reflect seasonal changes in land and air prices.

Validity—This ticket is valid for specific dates specified. Since land services are reserved, there is no flexibility.

Purchase—Tickets must be paid for at least 15 days before the departure of European flights and 5 days before departure to the Middle East. This does not mean seats will be available on the deadline. Always plan ahead during the peak season.

Restrictions—You must fly to and from your destination with the *same* group of passengers. While on the ground, you may travel independently. Your travel agent or tour operator will form the group.

Land Purchase requirements—Basic package in Europe—$70 minimum purchase is required; in Middle East and Israel—$45 minimum.

Stopovers—They are permitted with these stipulations: Europe—one stopover is permitted for an extra $10. Middle East—one stopover is permitted for an extra $25.

Savings—40 percent over regular coach fare.

CHILDREN'S FARE

A child is charged 50 percent of GIT adult fare.

EXCEPTIONS TO GIT 7–8-DAY TOUR

Europe—Stay requirements are seven days minimum, eight days maximum.

Middle East—Stay requirements are four days minimum, eight days maximum.

Note: The group is formed by a travel agent or tour operator. You do not have to concern yourself with the group's formation. The only worry here would be if the group did not materialize. Ask your agent what the chances are for such a problem.

14–21-DAY GIT TOURS

This package has the same basic structure as its short-term version, the 7–8-day tour. Below we list the *differences* in requirements between the two.

Land Purchase Requirements—Europe—$120 minimum purchase for 14-day stay; $10 more for each day over 14. Middle East—$70 minimum purchase for entire stay.

Stopovers—They are permitted with these stipulations: Europe—two *free* and two at $10 each are allowed. Middle East—six *free* stopovers are allowed.

The weekend surcharge is in effect for 14–21-day tours. Eastbound passengers are charged an additional $15 on Friday and Saturday. Westbound passengers are charged an additional $15 on Saturday and Sunday.

EXCEPTIONS TO 14–21-DAY TOUR

Europe—14-day minimum, 21-day maximum stay requirements, except:

Italy—seven-day minimum, 14-day maximum in basic season, 10-day minimum, 21-day maximum in peak season.

Portugal and Greece—7-day minimum stay and 21-day maximum stay requirements.

BUDGET FARES

This is the newest fare to emerge. It is in direct response to Laker and the whole deregulation policy. It is sold under the following conditions:

1. Passengers reserve and pay for a flight 21 days before the Sunday of the week they wish to fly (you pick the week—the airline picks the day and hour).
2. About 10 days before the flight, you are notified of the time and day you have been given a seat.
3. If you cancel your reservation, you are penalized $50 or more.

Seasons—Eastbound peak runs till September 3. Westbound peak runs until October 1. Fares reflect seasonal fluctuations.

Validity—Ticket is good for up to one year (although you are not really sure a seat will be available).

Stopovers—None.

Savings—59 percent off regular coach fares.

STANDBY FARES

This is a student favorite and is now available to all patient and hearty passengers. It is sold under these conditions:

1. Three hours before the scheduled departure of a flight, standby tickets go on sale. (Lines often form many hours earlier.)
2. Tickets are sold for regularly scheduled flights that have empty seats; so seating is limited.
3. Always call airline for definite times, regulations and predictions of seat availability.

Seasons—Eastbound peak runs until September 3. Westbound until October 1. Fares reflect seasonal fluctuations.

Validity—Ticket is valid for one year (although you are not really sure a seat will be available).

Stopovers—None.

Savings—59 percent off regular coach fare.

CHARTER FARES
AND CHARTER GROUPS

The introduction of charter air travel has been the single most important change in air transport in the last three decades. By making low round trip fares available to everyone who can plan far enough ahead to meet the advanced purchase requirements, air travel is no longer the privilege of the wealthy few.

There have been many problems with the charter method. Twenty-five percent of all charters are canceled some time between ticket purchase and takeoff. Fly-by-night charter companies have sprung up, snatched their passengers' money and disappeared. Bad planning has stranded thousands of travelers in strange airports with no tickets, no planes and no way home. There have been mistakes and intentional frauds. But in the last few years the government has imposed new regulations on the charter companies and the regularly scheduled airlines (like TWA) have entered the charter field, bringing up the general level of service and dependability. There is no place on the globe that is not served by charter flights at least some part of the year.

Even though the charter business is better regulated and more dependable than it used to be, there are several things that you, the consumer, should do to make sure you get the most reliable services possible.

Always shop around. Find out what is available. There are many different types of charters offered to any destination. Find out what aircraft the charter company will be using, who supplies them, and how long the charter company has been conducting business.

When buying land arrangements with your flight, find out everything about the accommodations. Do you have a choice of hotels? What are the rooms like? Are they conveniently located? Do you get discounts on sight-seeing tours? Do you get everywhere you want to go? It is possible that a more expensive package gives you much more for your money in terms of comfort, dependability and sight-seeing activities. Don't be taken in by promises of cheap paradises.

Consider your destination carefully. The cost of charters to London or Madrid is very low. The cost to Athens is considerably higher. Where are you going to travel? Is it cheaper to go on land from Spain to Greece—and to see the sights—than to fly to Athens directly and miss the rest of Europe?

As we have cautioned several times already, always buy cancellation insurance! This is the single most important thing you can do before you travel. Cancellation insurance should be offered to you on your charter contract. This insurance will protect you from paying the cancellation penalty that is levied if for any reason you cannot make your flight.

OTC—ONE STOP INCLUSIVE TOUR CHARTERS

These are deceptively named. They permit more than one stopover. They are explained in detail in the Domestic Fares section.

Purchase—there is no longer an advanced purchase requirement. But since charters sell quickly, you are advised to purchase your tickets as early as possible. Some European countries still require advance purchase, so check with your travel agent or charter company well ahead of time.

Land Purchase Requirements—$15 per day for adults and $7.50 for children (2–11 years old).

Minimum stay requirements—you must be away at least seven days. The maximum length varies from two weeks to two months.

Reliability—OTCs may be canceled by the charter operator any time up to 15 days before departure. Therefore, you should check with your charter company at that time to make sure you still have a flight!

Cancellation policy—If you cancel your reservation, you are subject to stiff penalties. Buy cancellation insurance.

ABC—ADVANCED BOOKING CHARTER

This is one of the most useful fares to be developed. It is an air-fare-only round trip, available from travel agents and tour operators. It applies to flights that are scheduled for departure and return on specific, non-transferable dates.

Seasons—Prices reflect seasons. "Peak" summer months are most expensive, the dead of winter is the cheapest.

Validity—The ABC is good for the specific dates specified at purchase.

Purchase—Tickets for ABCs must be paid 45 days in advance for flights to Europe. Other locations—15–30 days in advance.

Restrictions—Europe—Minimum stay of seven days is required. Cancellation penalties can be 100 percent of your fare if you give the company last-minute notice, and they cannot replace you.

Savings—*one-half* over regular coach. You could go twice for the price!

ITC—INCLUSIVE TOUR CHARTERS

This fare requires that you also purchase a minimum amount of land arrangements. The savings are good and the cost of the land packages *plus* the air fare is often only slightly higher than regular coach fare alone.

Note: This fare, so similar to the OTC's, will soon merge with that fare and, in due time, disappear altogether.

Seasons—The prices of air fare and land services reflect the changes in seasonal demands.

Validity—Ticket is good for specific dates of charter flight only. Nontransferable.

Purchase—No advance purchase is required. This does not mean it is always available, but it does give the last-minute traveler a chance to take advantage of the new discount fares.

Restrictions—Stopovers *are required!* You must stop in three cities overnight, each one at least 50 miles from the others.

Land Purchase Requirements—The *total* package must equal 110 percent of the normal coach air fare.

Minimum Stay Requirements—You must be abroad for at least seven days.

TIPS, HINTS AND LISTS

Companies such as American Express, Arthur Frommer and Thomas Cook offer a wide range of tours and charter flights. They generally charter planes from regularly scheduled airlines such as TWA or KLM or use the largest and most dependable of the "unscheduled" lines. Their accommodations are well explained and their brochures are informative. However, they are the most ordinary way to go. They often fail to offer innovative tours. Their costs are high. You get *and* give up a lot. So, ask yourself what you need and what you want before you sign up with one of these granddaddy of tours.

—Always check with the national airline of the country you will be visiting. Often they can give you excellent deals on air/land packages. They are promoting their own country and, therefore, are eager to have you as a customer.

—Read all literature carefully. You can gather a lot of information from the brochures the airline puts out. But *beware!* The beautiful color photos can be deceptive. Have a travel agent check the "World Hotel Guide" for information on the accommodations. You should find out its location, size and rating before you arrive.

—Make a list of all expenses that are not included in your land package. Tips, airport taxes, land transportation, meals etc., can all add enormously to the cost of your great discount vacation. If the out-of-pocket expenses are too high, you might do better with a more expensive but more all-inclusive package.

—Ask about the type of aircraft and the seating arrangements. You know that charters are crowded, but how crowded? Some charters now fly 747s; others stuff you into DC-8s. Know before you go.

And last but *not least,* read every word in your contract.

You have only yourself to blame if you are surprised by some unexpected expense or restriction just because you didn't take the time to read the small print.

HOT TIPS

The best intra-European tour company we know is Thompson's Holidays of London. They offer trips from England to southern Europe *plus* hotel accommodations for *less* than half of the regular air fare alone. You can throw out the land arrangements and still save money.

For information about their tours write Thompson's Holidays, Greater London House, Hampstead Road, London N.W.1, England or M.S. Marketing, 516 Fifth Avenue, New York, New York 10036.

One of the most useful guides to charter, discount and excursion fares is: Jen Jurgen's *Charter Flight Directory and Guide to Other Air Travel Bargains.* You can obtain it for $4.95, by writing to Travel Information Bureau, P.O. Box 105, Kings Park, New York 11754.

There are many such tours and charters available for travel *within Europe only.* Until now it has been almost impossible to find out what was available. There is a new regulation that requires travel agents to inform travelers of such discount fares *upon request.* If your agent has no information, contact the national airline of the country you will be visiting or the National Tourist Board; they should be able to help you.

The best sources of charter information are generally available at travel agencies. If your local agent does not have *Jax Fax*, a publication devoted to listing all available charters, write to the publication directly at 280 Tokeneke Road, Darien, Connecticut 06820.

Do Not Overlook These Sources of Information!

CHAPTER SIX
THE AIRLINES

No matter what your destination—New York to Chicago, or Orlando to Milano—there are many airlines from which to choose your flight. How you make those choices should be determined by what you know about each airline: its flight schedules, its services, its performance records and what you want an airline to provide for you.

In this chapter we provide a look at all the major or "trunk" airlines that serve large metropolitan airports in the U.S. and abroad. We have also included a look at the most important foreign airline companies. When you become aware of the services provided by each airline, you can make the wisest selection for your next trip.

Another feature of this chapter is a look at two leading consumer surveys and what they reveal to be the least-liked airlines and aircraft. And the *best*, too.

Put all this information together and you have one more way to make sure you get the most out of your travel dollar and travel fun!

CONSUMER SURVEYS

The two surveys that follow are in agreement about several of their findings. Although a travel experience is often a subjective one, the surveys provide a general outline of the tastes of the American flying public.

THE AIRLINE PASSENGERS ASSOCIATION

This organization surveyed its 38,255 members (and received 12,980 replies) in 1977. The results are given below. (For detailed information about the organization itself, see chapter four.)

MOST AVOIDED AIRLINE—DOMESTIC

1. Eastern
2. Allegheny
3. Braniff

MOST FAVORED AIRLINE—DOMESTIC

1. American
2. United
3. Delta

AIRCRAFT PREFERRED ON SHORT FLIGHTS—LESS THAN TWO HOURS

1. Boeing 727
2. McDonnell Douglas DC-10
3. Boeing 747

AIRCRAFT AVOIDED ON SHORT FLIGHTS

1. McDonnell Douglas DC-9
2. Boeing 747
3. McDonnell Douglas DC-8

AIRCRAFT PREFERRED ON FLIGHTS OF MORE THAN THREE HOURS

1. Boeing 747
2. McDonnell Douglas DC-10 (a distant second)
3. Lockheed L1011 (an even more distant third)

AIRCRAFT AVOIDED ON FLIGHTS OF THREE HOURS OR MORE

1. Boeing 727
2. McDonnell Douglas DC-8
3. Boeing 707

THE TRAVEL ADVISOR

This publication is a monthly newsletter for frequent (or serious) travelers. It touches on all aspects of travel and is full of advice on airlines, accommodations and important tips on the best deals and the worst facilities available worldwide. *TA* publishes the results of its annual reader survey. The results follow.

If you want more information on this interesting organization write *The Travel Advisor*, 141 Parkway Road, Suite 18, Bronxville, New York, 10708.

WHAT ARE THE BEST U.S. AIRLINES?

1. American
2. United
3. TWA
4. Eastern
5. Pan Am

WHAT ARE THE BEST FOREIGN AIRLINES?

1. Swissair
2. Japan Air Lines
3. Delta
4. Scandinavian Airlines
5. Continental
6. Western

U.S. PASSENGER AIRLINES

This list of U.S. carriers and their overall route miles is provided to show you the relative size of each airline. The miles given represent an approximation of the total (sometimes duplicated) route miles that each airline flies between all the airports in its network. (Statistics taken from *FAA Statistical Handbook of Aviation*, U.S. Department of Transportation, Federal Aviation Administration, 1976.)

Domestic Trunk Lines	Overall Route Miles
United	47,805
Delta	45,104
American	42,884
Eastern	42,456
National	30,090
TWA	28,099
Western	27,054
Continental	25,955
Braniff	20,261

International Trunk Lines	Overall Route Miles
Pan Am	267,540
TWA	78,196
Braniff	32,300
Northwest	23,680
Eastern	23,569
American	21,108
Continental/Air Micronesia	14,602
Delta	8,855
Western	6,642
National	4,451

Domestic Feeder Lines	Overall Route Miles
Frontier	11,445
Southern	9,089
Allegheny	6,543
North Central	6,231
Hughes Air West	5,916
Ozark	5,765
Texas International	5,562
Piedmont	3,909
Air New England	797

UNITED AIRLINES

As the name indicates, United is a company formed from the merger of several smaller, pioneering airlines. In 1939 when the name United came into being, Boeing Transport and National Transport were joined together. Boeing, which flew a mail run from San Francisco to Chicago accepted passengers—if they sat on mail sacks—and charged them $200 for the privilege. National completed the transcontinental run from Chicago to New York. Passengers were taken on board for an additional $200 and were seated on a mail sack in the open cockpit of the plane, wearing a parachute and goggles!

Routes: United has 47,805 route miles and flies to 30 states all across the country, covering all areas except the Northern Midwest and some Southwestern localities. Authorization for new routes is being sought—they would include a Seattle–Tokyo run, a New Orleans–Cancun run and a California–Montreal run.

Service: Including Vancouver and Toronto, Canada, United flies to 110 cities.

Aircraft: The United fleet is composed of:

    59 Boeing 737
   107 Boeing 727-100
    28 Boeing 727-200
    18 Boeing 727-200A
    18 Boeing 747
    56 McDonnell Douglas DC-8
    37 McDonnell Douglas DC-10

Volume: United is Number One in the U.S. It carried 34,384,000 passengers in 1977.

Special services: United provides various special services for its passengers. The most common services are special meals and certain medical accommodations. Although United has many services, it does not indulge in a great number of promotions but is a good all-around airline—the biggest in the country—and it concentrates on getting you where you're going as smoothly as possible.

Meals are provided for those passengers who have special dietary, health, religious or personal needs. Each year more than 60,000 Kosher meals and 150,000 other special meals are prepared. Order your special meal at least 24 hours before departure. (A note of interest: United Kitchens make 90,000 meals a day!)

Handicapped services and provisions are standard. If you have any special medical needs, always inform your travel agent or ticket clerk well ahead of time, so all arrangements for early boarding, comfortable seating, on-board attention and airport routine can be made.

Wheelchair reservations should be made at the same time as ticket reservations.

Check-in requirements are consistent with U.S. regulations and international requirements.

EASTERN AIR LINES

Eastern's network covers a large area, with service originating in New York, Atlanta, Miami, to cities throughout the North and Southwest and the Central and Eastern United States. Internationally, Eastern flies to Toronto, Montreal and Ottawa in Canada and Mexico City and Acapulco in Mexico. In the Carribean, Eastern flies to 15 localities.

Service: All told, Eastern flies to 91 airports in 28 states and the District of Columbia, and to 20 international airports.

Aircraft: The *Eastern* fleet is composed of:

Regular Service:
67 McDonnell Douglas
   DC-9-30
53 Boeing 727-200
32 Lockheed L-1011
46 Boeing 727-100
9 McDonnell Douglas DC-9-50
24 Boeing 727
9 McDonnell Douglas DC-9-10
14 Electra
4 Airbus A300 B

Shuttle Service:
2 Boeing 727
8 McDonnell Douglas
   DC-9-30
15 Electra Propjets

Volume: Eastern carried 31,582,000 passengers in 1977, making it the second largest air carrier in the U.S.

Special services: Eastern provides various special services for its passengers. The most common are special meals and certain medical accommodations. In addition, Eastern has its own unique services that distinguish it from all the others.

Shuttle service: Eastern provides shuttle service between New York and Washington, D.C., and between New York and Boston. Unlike any air plan in the country, it features hourly departures from La Guardia in New York; no reservations *ever;* ticket purchased *on board* flight; payment accepted in cash, check or credit card; *guaranteed* seating. Eastern will *always* get you on the flight you want. They assure this by having planes on standby. If one is filled, another is brought into service.

Note: The reason the aircraft in the Eastern fleet are separated into regular and shuttle service is because there are *no classes* on shuttle and seating is much denser than on regular planes.

Leisure class: This is another Eastern special service. Eastern has a full explanation of it in its timetable and encourages its use. The special rules governing this fare are explained below.

Purchase a ticket on a flight at the regular coach price. Ticket is designated leisure.

This is usually done on crowded, sold-out or oversold flights, when last-minute passage is important.

Report to check-in gate at least 20 minutes ahead of flight's departure.

If Eastern cannot honor your ticket because no seat becomes available, they will *refund* the entire ticket price *immediately and fly you free* on the next available flight.

Note: In this day of overbooking, this looks like a good way for a gambler to fly.

Note: This offer is not valid if the plane is grounded because of weather, equipment failure or government intervention.

Meals are available for passengers with special dietary, religious or personal needs if they are ordered at least eight hours before scheduled departure of the flight. (The Eastern menu is somewhat more limited than many airlines, providing only seven different selections.)

Handicapped services and provisions are standard. All medical needs can be dealt with on an individual basis. Contact your Eastern representative early if you need special boarding, medical attention, oxygen or preferred seating.

Wheelchair reservations are available at airports when arranged at the time you make your reservation.

Check-in requirements—The times listed in the Eastern timetable are *stricter* than the basic law. Eastern asks passengers on *domestic* flights to be at the boarding gate at least 40 minutes before departure. On *international* flights they request you arrive at the gate 60 minutes before departure.

DELTA AIR LINES

Delta Air Lines began in 1925 as a crop-dusting outfit; the first passengers were transported in 1929; eventually, through a process of acquisition of the old Chicago & Southern Air Lines and the Northeast Airlines, Delta became one of the U.S.'s major passenger carriers.

Routes: Delta flies from Maine to the southernmost tip of Florida, stopping throughout the East Coast. Its newest domestic routes are between Atlanta and Denver and between Memphis and Tampa. The network extends into California, Illinois and Texas. Internationally, Delta serves the Caribbean, Bermuda, Canada, Venezuela, and now London (from Atlanta only).

Service: Delta flies to 90 cities in 29 states, 6 countries and one territory. Its routes cover 37,745 miles.

Aircraft: The Delta fleet is composed of:

30 Lockheed L-1011
13 McDonnell Douglas Super DC-8
10 McDonnell Douglas Standard DC-8
124 Boeing 727
53 McDonnell Douglas Super DC-9

Volume: Delta flew 30,553,000 passengers in 1977, making it the third largest airline in the U.S.

Special services: Delta provides special services for its passengers. The most common features are special meals and certain medical accommodations. In addition, Delta features special promotional plans and tends to emphasize short-term offerings for in-flight services and air/land packages to its southern resort areas.

Meals are available to those people who have special dietary, health, religious or personal needs if requested when the ticket reservation is made. Coach flights to Florida offer a special menu of steak and champagne as a promotional gimmick. Nice gimmick!

Handicapped services and provisions are standard. Delta requests that all special arrangements be made at least 24 hours before the scheduled departure of your flight. For particularly delicate medical needs, be sure to give more time. Your travel agent or ticket agent will help you make the plans.

Wheelchair reservations are available 24 hours before scheduled departure also. Delta will provide a chair at the point of departure and arrival.

Check-in requirements are stricter than required by law. Delta reserves the right to *cancel* your reservation if you are not at the gate at least 10 minutes before the departure of your domestic flight and 30 minutes before the departure of your international flight.

AMERICAN AIRLINES

American was formed in 1930 with the merger of many small airline companies into one large concern. Charles Lindbergh was a pilot for one of the formative companies, Robertson Air. In 1926 he flew a DeHavilland DH-4 biplane on a pioneering mail run from St. Louis to Chicago. That route was expanded and developed until it became one of the main air links in the country, even if it was necessary to make *ten* stops between the two cities for fuel, rest and safety!

Routes: Today American flies from coast to coast and from Canada to Mexico. The Northwest and the Upper Midwest are the two sections of the U.S. not served. Internationally, American flies to Canada, Mexico and the Caribbean.

Service: American serves 42 cities with its domestic flights and 28 cities on its international routes.

Aircraft: The American fleet is composed of:

43 Boeing 707-123B
10 Boeing 707-323B
20 Boeing 707-323C
25 McDonnell Douglas DC-10
8 Boeing 747
70 Boeing 727-223
57 Boeing 727-023

Volume: American carried 24,295,000 passengers in 1977, making it the fourth largest airline in the U.S.

Special services: American provides various special services for its passengers. The most common are special meals and certain medical accommodations. In addition, American has its own unique services that distinguish it from all others.

Transcontinental extras offered are advanced seat reservations on many domestic flights; extra gate personnel to assist passengers at boarding gate to speed up boarding time; choice of entree on lunch and dinner in both first and coach classes.

Meals for those who have special dietary, health, religious or personal needs are available if ordered at the time reservations are made. Ask the airline ticket clerk for a complete list of choices on your flight.

Handicapped services and provisions are excellent! American is very responsive to the needs of the handicapped in travel and is one of the leaders in handling and arranging for transportation of large groups of handicapped tourists.

Wheelchair reservations are taken at the same time as ticket reservations. The airline will arrange for a wheelchair in the airport from which you depart and at your destination.

Special unlisted reservation numbers are available to help you make faster reservations. Anyone may use them but they are particularly helpful to those making special arrangements or needing special attention. They are as follows:

Boston 542-6566
Buffalo 856-4143
Chicago 782-8628
Cincinnati 621-3665
Dallas/Fort Worth
  267-3777
Detroit 965-0870
Los Angeles 937-7580
New York 661-8230
Phoenix 264-2574
San Francisco 433-2880
Toronto 925-2108
Washington, D.C.
  393-2377

A *Special* seating chart guide to all American aircraft is available on request.

Check-in requirements are standard.

Note: American now has city check-in which allows you to confirm your reservation, select a seat and receive a boarding pass before departing for the airport. There is no waiting at check-in counters. Ask your airline or travel agent for details when you make your reservation.

Special Note: American is not only found to be the consistent favorite of the American flying public, but it is also the most dependable. The Flight Safety Foundation awarded American a citation for "Distinguished Performance" in recognition of six million hours of safe flying time achieved over a ten-year period. Since that award, American has tragically had an accident, but, overall, it remains a remarkable airline for service and safety.

TRANS WORLD AIRLINES

TWA was a pioneer in transcontinental air travel. In the late Twenties, the journey from coast to coast had to be made on plane/rail connections because the problems of night flying had not been solved. Passengers would get off one plane at dusk, board a train for the night, and hook up with another waiting plane in the morning. This went on for 48 hours! It took almost a decade to get the journey down to a gruelling 16 hours, all by airplane.

Routes: TWA flies from Boston to Los Angeles and Miami to Chicago and many, many points in between. Internationally, TWA flies to Athens, Bahrein, the Azores, Barcelona, Cairo, Casablanca, Dublin, Geneva, Lisbon, London, Madrid, Malaga, Milan, Nice/Monte Carlo, Paris, Rome, Santa Maria, Shannon and Tel Aviv.

Service: TWA flies to a total of 57 cities worldwide.

Aircraft: The TWA fleet is composed of:

    9 Boeing 747
24 Lockheed L-1011
88 Boeing 707
71 Boeing 727
13 McDonnell Douglas DC-9

Volume: TWA carried 17,776,000 passengers in 1977. This figure does not include its extensive charter service. It is the fifth largest airline in the U.S.

Special services: TWA provides various special services for its passengers. The most common are special meals and certain medical accommodations. In addition, TWA has its own unique services, including the following:

Round-trip Check-in service is offered by TWA (as well as a growing number of other airlines). You can get your seat assignment for both outbound and return flights at the same time and may also select your seat as much as 28 days in advance. This makes it necessary to wait in the airport check-in line *once* instead of *twice.*

Budget and Standby fares are now available (thanks to Freddie Laker) from New York to London and Rome. The budget fare is purchased 21 days before the *week* you want to fly. You are assigned a flight during that week at the discretion of the airline. Return trips are confirmed in a similar fashion. Cancellation penalty: $50 New York to London and 50 percent of your fare New York to Rome.

Standby provides no advanced reservation, no need for

advanced payment and no cancellation penalties. Tickets are sold, as available, three hours before each flight. There is no standby available to Rome. The price is the same as for a budget ticket.

Meals are provided for those who have special dietary, health, religious or personal needs. Make a reservation for your special meal when you make your reservation.

Handicapped services and provisions are excellent. TWA's booklet, *Air Travel for the Handicapped*, is very complete. Ask for it at your travel agent's or airline ticket office. Any special needs will be met if enough time is allowed. You should always inform your travel agent or ticket clerk of your medical requirements. Even temporarily disabled travelers with broken limbs, etc., may take advantage of early boarding, special seating and prearranged in-flight services.

Wheelchair reservations are available for your arrival and departure if requested at time ticket reservation is made. Special seating chart guides to all TWA aircraft are available on request, to help you make your seat selection.

Special Notes: TWA publishes excellent brochures on international travel. They are readable, informative and helpful. Always investigate.

Check-in requirements conform to U.S. law and standard international specifications. In foreign airports check to see what regulations apply, to avoid needlessly jeopardizing your reservation.

ALLEGHENY AIRLINES

Allegheny is a truly successful "small" airline. Founded in 1938, Allegheny was a mail carrier until 1949, when it took on passengers. In 1968 it merged with Lake Central and then in 1972 with Mohawk.

Routes: Allegheny's route includes two international stops in Montreal and Toronto; it flies as far south as Memphis and as far west as Minneapolis. It has extensive route expansion plans—so keep your eye on this airline!

Service: Allegheny flies to 18 states and Canada and serves 100 cities all over the Northeast and Central U.S.

Aircraft: The Allegheny fleet is composed of:

    8 McDonnell Douglas DC-9-50
   41 McDonnell Douglas DC-9-31
   10 Boeing 727-100
   31 BAC 1-11 Fan Jets

Volume: Allegheny flew 11,653,000 passengers in 1977, making it the sixth busiest airline in the U.S.

Special services: Allegheny provides special services for its passengers. The most common are special meals and certain medical accommodations. In addition, Allegheny has special features that distinguish it from the others.

Commuter service: The Allegheny Commuter program, now in its eleventh year, is a unique concept designed to provide smaller, low traffic-producing cities with the best possible commercial air service. Increased flight frequency, prime-time scheduling and excellent dependability are among the features. The service is available to 37 cities, including Altoona, Pennsylvania; Watertown, Maine; Terre Haute, Indiana and the aircraft involved carry from 15-30 passengers.

Meals for those with special dietary, health, religious or personal needs are available if requested in advance; however, Allegheny flights are usually not long enough for a meal to be served.

Handicapped services and provisions are standard. Contact your travel agent or ticket clerk to make arrangements for any special needs. Plan ahead.

Wheelchair reservations can be made at the same time as ticket reservations.

NORTHWEST ORIENT

Northwest Orient has always been a pioneer of international air routes. Since 1927 when it flew its first passengers—106 in the entire year—it has led the way in over-the-pole navigation.

Routes: In the U.S. Northwest serves Florida, Louisiana, the Northeast, California and the Northwest. In the Orient, it flies to the Philippines, Hong Kong and Japan. Its new routes to Europe take it to Bergen, Copenhagen, Glasgow, Goteborg, Helsinki, Oslo, Reykjavik, Stavanger and Stockholm.

Service: The total number of cities served by Northwest is 55—39 in the U.S. and 16 abroad.

Aircraft: The Northwest fleet is composed of:

    34 Boeing 727-100
    31 Boeing 727-200
     2 Boeing 707-320
    20 Boeing 747
    22 McDonnell Douglas DC-10

Volume: Northwest flew 10,355,000 passengers in 1977, making it the seventh busiest airline in the U.S.

Special services: Northwest provides special services for its passengers. The most common are special meals and certain medical accommodations. In addition, Northwest has special features that distinguish it from the others.

VIP Travel Plan is an example of the full-fare coach service described in chapter three under Domestic Coach Class. This service is provided to the traveler who pays full coach fare. Because so many discount fares are available (and because those paying far less than full fare get to sit with those paying full fare), some airlines have started this program to make the coach customer feel like he is not getting ripped off. (There is good reason to feel that he is!) The conditions of this program are described below:

1. Reserve a seat in a special coach seating area when you make your reservation. Seating is limited, and it is on a first-come, first-served basis.
2. No children are allowed to sit in the private coach section.

3. A special movie is shown to coach passengers.

4. A special food service is offered—somewhat less than first-class but better than the rest of the plane.

5. Special arrangements with Oriental hotels and shops can be made at the time of reservation that entitle you to discounts on rooms and purchases.

Meals for those with special dietary, health, religious or personal needs are available if requested at least 24 hours before the scheduled departure of the flight.

Handicapped services and provisions are standard. Contact your travel agent or ticket clerk to make arrangements for any special needs. Plan ahead.

Wheelchair reservations can be made at the same time as ticket reservations.

Check-in requirements: Northwest asks that you be at the gate 20 minutes ahead of time for domestic flights and 40 minutes ahead of time for international flights. They reserve the right to *cancel* your reservation if you do not check in at least 10 minutes before domestic flights and 40 minutes before international departures.

BRANIFF INTERNATIONAL AIRLINES

Beginning as a small southwestern airline, Braniff made its first passenger flight in 1928 on a hop from Tulsa to Oklahoma City. As one of the pioneers of the South American routes, it followed Pan Am into the heart of that continent in 1948.

Routes: In continental U.S., Braniff flies from Atlanta to Honolulu, from New York to the West Coast and throughout Florida. Its routes cover the South and Southwest and extend from Chicago to Dallas/Fort Worth, the hub of its system. Internationally, Braniff flies to Rio, São Paulo, Asunción, Buenos Aires, Santiago, La Paz, Guayaquil, Lima, Quito, Cali and Bogotá. Its newest route is from Dallas/Fort Worth to London.

Aircraft: The Braniff fleet is composed of:

2 Boeing 747

84 Boeing 727 (of various configurations)
14 McDonnell Douglas DC-8

Volume: Braniff flew more than 9,814,000 passengers in 1977. It is the eighth largest airline in the U.S.

Special services: All airlines provide certain special features for their passengers. The most common features are special meals and certain medical accommodations. In addition, each airline features special promotional plans that make it distinct from the others. Braniff's package tours of South America are well priced and interesting. And they have planes painted by Calder for an aesthetic flying experience!

Full-Fare Economy Cabin—On 747 flights to Europe, Braniff offers a special section for passengers who pay full coach fares. More comfortable seating, quieter surroundings, choice of entrees, extra on-board storage areas, and better service are among the special features. If you fly full coach, make sure you request this section. Seating is limited and you need to make your reservations early.

Meals are provided for those passengers with special dietary, health, religious or personal needs if such requests are made at the time you make your ticket reservation.

Handicapped services and provisions are standard in the U.S. and can be minimal abroad. Rio's new airport is built with moving sidewalks, ramps, etc., but elsewhere in South America, you can expect little help. In the U.S., all accommodations can be made with advanced notice.

Wheelchair reservations can be made at the time of ticket reservation. Talk to your travel agent or ticket clerk for all arrangements.

Note: Braniff is seeking vast changes in its routes and services, including use of Concorde service and authorization to fly to Tokyo.

Check-in requirements are stricter than required by law. On international flights, Braniff will not honor your reservation unless you are at the point of "ticket liftline" (that's a quote from the timetable!) 30 minutes before scheduled departure; it's five minutes for domestic flights.

WESTERN AIRLINES

Since its beginning as a small mail carrier with passengers seated on top of the mail sacks, Western has introduced many innovations. The first in-flight meals were served on a Western flight, and stewardesses were used on Western long before most other airlines. Today Western has an excellent record for service and performance.

Routes: Western flies from Anchorage to Honolulu and from Vancouver to Mexico City, covering the western U.S. from Butte to Phoenix. Its eastern flights include Miami and Minneapolis. (Some of its routes are now interchangeable with Continental and Braniff.)

Service: Western flies to 44 cities in the U.S. and to Canada and Mexico.

Aircraft: The Western fleet is composed of:

9 McDonnell Douglas DC-10
5 Boeing 707-300C
8 Boeing 720-B
28 Boeing 727-200
23 Boeing 737-200

Volume: Western flew 9,395,000 passengers in 1977, making it the ninth largest airline in the U.S.

Special services: Western provides special services for its passengers. The most common are special meals and certain medical accommodations. In addition Western is known for its service, plus champagne flights, good on time records and all-around top-notch procedures.

Meals are provided for those passengers with special dietary, religious, health or personal needs if requested when ticket reservation is made.

Handicapped services and provisions are standard. All provisions must be made when you make your reservation. Your travel agent or ticket clerk will help you arrange for early boarding, in-flight attention, special seating, etc.

Wheelchair reservations are available at time of ticket reservations.

Check-in: Western specifies that you must check in for a *domestic* flight 30 minutes before departure and for an *international* flight 45 minutes before departure.

CONTINENTAL AIR LINES

Although not well known all over the country, Continental has been an important western airline since 1933. Its first plane was a Lockheed Vega, a four-passenger craft used for mail and passenger service. Today it is a vital air link throughout the entire Pacific and the western U.S.

Routes: Continental serves the entire West from Chicago and Miami. Its newest routes take it into Denver from Miami and Tampa and from Los Angeles to Sydney via Honolulu, Samoa, Fiji and New Zealand. In the Pacific it serves Japan and the surrounding islands.

Aircraft: The Continental fleet is composed of:

42 Boeing 727 (including two
    for its affiliate Air Micronesia)
15 McDonnell Douglas DC-10

Volume: Continental/Air Micronesia flew a total of 8,248,000 passengers in 1977, making it the tenth largest airline in the U.S. today.

Special services: Continental provides various special services for its passengers. The most common services are special meals and certain medical accommodations. Continental does not run big promotional campaigns because of its regional emphasis. Its package tours are offered throughout the Pacific.

Commuter service is the Continental California special! Within that state, special routes, discounts and fare plans are offered.

Discount "basic" fares have been introduced, as is the trend these days. Continental requires no prepayment, that each of its DC-10s have at least 27 discount seats available, that each of its 727s have at least 16 discount seats available, all discount seats be located in the back of the plane.

Handicapped services and provisions are standard. No special emphasis is put on serving the handicapped to date. You can arrange for all special medical needs when you make your reservation, and Continental will do whatever possible to assist you. If you are flying into small airports, you must be particularly cautious. It is difficult to get the same facilities as in larger metropolitan airports and extra time may be needed to work out arrangements.

Wheelchairs are available on request at all airports.

PAN AMERICAN WORLD AIRWAYS

Pan Am, the flagship of the American airline fleet, has been the U.S. representative to the world since 1927, when Pan Am became the first American company to enter the international market. Pan Am has led the industry in pioneering routes and advancing technological innovations. Nevertheless, the company has had some very hard years financially. Passenger load has declined and some say service is less than satisfactory.

Routes: Pan Am flies over 200,000 miles from Ghana to Guam and from New York to Nairobi. Europe, Asia, the Orient, Africa and South America are all on the Pan Am flyway. Pan Am has not serviced domestic flights within the U.S., but recently it has been granted the right to fly passengers "on-line" to their points of international departure and to fly New York–Houston with a standby and a discount fare. They are being allowed to expand into the domestic market. The acquisition of National will let them obtain prime U.S. routes.

Service: Pan Am lands at 82 airports in 63 countries. In the U.S. it serves 14 cities.

Aircraft: The Pan Am Fleet is composed of:

> 40 Boeing 747 (including the 747SP, a smaller, wider, lighter aircraft with a flight range of 1,500 more miles than the standard 747)
> 45 Boeing 707 (9 for charter flights)
> 13 Boeing 727

Volume: Pan Am transported 7,647,000 passengers in 1977, making it the eleventh largest airline in the U.S.

Special services: Pan Am provides special services for its passengers. The most common are special meals and certain medical accommodations. In addition, Pan Am has certain promotional options that it provides to entice customers away from other airlines. Pan Am has gone into the charter and budget fare field extensively and is now in direct competition with Laker, with very low-priced fares from New York to London. It is also planning to institute cut-rate transpacific flights that would *halve* the price of a ticket from San Francisco to Tokyo! (We owe our thanks to Freddie Laker for making the other airlines begin to think like him!)

Budget fare—A fixed number of seats are available on each of Pan Am's three regularly scheduled flights to London's Heathrow Airport daily.

Three weeks ahead of *the week* you wish to depart, you make your reservation. You must pay at that time. Prices reflect seasonal peak and off-peak rates.

Seven days *before the week* you want to fly, Pan Am will tell you what flight you have been assigned to.

You *never* have a choice of day or time.

You *do get* all in-flight services—food, etc., just like a coach passenger.

Note: Seats are limited and go fast. Plan ahead.

Standby fare—A fixed number of seats are allowed to be sold as standby on each of Pan Am's three regularly scheduled flights to London's Heathrow Airport daily.

These seats are available only when the budget fare does *not* sell out all available seats. Budget has priority over standby.

*Tickets for standby go on sale three hours before the scheduled departure of the flight. Lines form much earlier than that. Tickets are sold on a first-come, first-served basis.

*Cost: The same as the budget fare—prices reflect seasonal peak and off-peak rates.

*You *do get* all-inflight services—food, etc., just like coach passengers.

Meals are available to all people with special dietary, religious, health or personal needs. Arrangements should be made when you make your ticket reservation.

Handicapped services are standard. Pan Am has no special literature in this area and offers no special advice. You should, therefore, leave ample time before your flight for all arrangements to be made. Check with your travel agent or ticket clerk for information.

Wheelchairs can be reserved if requested 48 hours before scheduled departure of your flight. Contact your travel agent or ticket clerk for information.

Check-in requirements are standard within the U.S. International airports have widely varying requirements. Always check with the airline or your travel agent before you leave.

NATIONAL AIRLINES

National began as a small regional airline. Today it is an important link between the East Coast and the sun spots of the South and West. Its newest ventures take it across the Atlantic. Not only has it acquired its own international flight but it is merging with Pan Am and will be a sister line to Pan Am's vast international routes.

Routes: National's own air network flies from Fort Lauderdale to San Francisco, from New England to New Orleans and from the South to London, Paris, Amsterdam and Frankfurt.

Service: In the U.S., National flies to 19 cities; abroad, to four.

Aircraft: The National fleet is composed of:

    38 Boeing 727
    15 McDonnell Douglas DC-10

Volume: National flew 6,225,000 passengers in 1977,

making it the twelfth largest airline in the U.S. (It is interesting to compare National with Pan Am. Pan Am flew only 1.5 million more passengers in 1977 but had to support an enormous fleet of planes and deal with airports in 82 cities instead of 23!)

Special services: National provides special services for its passengers. The most common are special meals and certain medical accommodations. In addition, National has its own promotional offerings that set it apart from the others. National specializes in vacation packages to Florida and the Southwest. Check its offerings if you are flying to those vacation spots.

Meals will be provided to passengers with special dietary, religious, health or personal needs with 24 hours' advanced notice.

Handicapped services and provisions are standard. Consult your travel agent or ticket clerk well ahead of your departure for information about what kinds of arrangements can be made.

Wheelchair service is available. Request it when you reserve your ticket.

Check-in requirements are stricter than the law requires. International passengers are asked to check in at least 45 minutes before scheduled departure. Domestic passengers should be at the check-in at least 10 minutes before departure.

FOREIGN PASSENGER AIRLINES

There are innumerable foreign airlines. We list the names and addresses of most of them in APPENDIX B. The bulk of American passengers traveling abroad will, however, depend on a few well-known international companies. The first section of this list covers the main IATA member airlines. The second part gives the outstanding points of those renegade companies such as Laker and Icelandic that offer regular service at low prices.

BRITISH AIRWAYS

British Airways has more unduplicated route miles—393,703—than any other airline in the world. From Anchorage to Auckland, British Airways visits 149 cities in 80 countries. South America and China are the only two parts of the globe it doesn't service. It transported 13,792,000 passengers in 1976.

Aircraft: The BA fleet of 208 aircraft is composed of:

```
 5  BAC Concorde Supersonic
25  Boeing 747
17  Boeing 707-336 and 436
15  VC-10 (Viscount is made by the
    British Aircraft Corporation.)
25  BAC111 (500 and 400)
 9  Tristars
25  Hawker Siddeley Trident Threes
56  Tridents (1, 1E, 2 and 3)
    and various Viscounts, Sikorsky
    and Merchantmen aircraft
```

Special services: British Airways provides special services to its passengers. The most common are special meals and certain medical provisions. In addition, each airline has its own special promotional plans that make it distinct from the others. British Airways is a specialist in tours of London and the British Isles. You can get remarkable packages for the theater, cars, country inns or city night life. If you're going to England, always look into British Airways offerings first.

The Concorde is the most special and most controversial of all BA's features. This new supersonic transport is an economic white elephant, a heavy beast that zips along at 1350+ m.p.h.! Other specifics include: Cost—$833 one way from London to New York; service—elegant continental feasting; seating—holds 100 passengers.

747 Executive Cabin service is the name British Airways gives to its full-fare coach service. It is available upon request when you make your reservation. The seating is separate from the rest of the passengers; it is quiet, child-free and better serviced. At the airport passengers have a separate check-in counter for faster service and priority baggage pickup at the point of arrival. Make sure you ask when you make your ticket reservation. The number of seats available is limited.

Budget and Standby fares on the New York to London run are available with the same conditions as Pan Am and TWA. Budget fare requires purchase three weeks in advance; standby, three hours. The fare is standard.

The timetable put out by BA is one of the best in the world. It gives information about the location, transportation to and cost of getting to local airports from all the cities it serves.

Brochures put out by BA are the best in the entire industry. You can find out everything you need to know about negotiating throughout England. They cover everything from baby-sitters (temporary nannies) to bus schedules. Collect all the literature and take it with you if you go to England.

Meals on regular BA flights are provided for passengers with special dietary, religious, health or personal needs if requested when ticket reservation is made.

Handicapped services and provisions are excellent. If you are in need of special attention en route or if you need to make plans for special boarding or seating, make sure you give your travel agent or ticket clerk enough time to make provisions. If you are going to be in London, ask for the BA brochure entitled *Shopping in London.* There you will find explanations of the layouts of all of London's main stores, highlighting wheelchair access, special restroom facilities, etc. Also, write for a copy of the brochure *London for the Disabled* from The Central Council of the Disabled, 35 Eccleston Square, London, England.

Wheelchairs are available at airports in Europe and the U.S. Elsewhere you should check with the airline. Make a reservation when you reserve your ticket.

Check-in requirements vary worldwide. See the BA timetable and always check with the ticket clerk.
Note: BA has a no-show penalty on flights outside the U.S. You may forfeit up to 25 percent of your ticket price if you do not call and cancel your flight.

IBERIA

Iberia, the Spanish national airline, has an extensive international route, covering 89 cities in 47 countries. From the U.S., it leaves New York and Miami for Europe and connecting flights around the world. From Europe, it flies to all parts of the globe except the Middle East and Asia. In 1977, 12,800,000 passengers flew on Iberia.

Aircraft: The Iberia fleet is composed of:

   3 Boeing 747
   6 DC-10
   7 McDonnell Douglas DC-8
 29 Boeing 727
 34 McDonnell Douglas DC-9
  7 Fairchild FH 227

Special services: Iberia has special meals and certain medical accommodations, in addition to promotions that distinguish it from other airlines. Iberia's charters and tours to Spain are its specialties.

Meals for passengers with special dietary, religious, health and personal needs are available if requested 24 hours before scheduled departure.

Handicapped services and provisions are standard to minimal. In New York all medical needs can be provided for with prior notice. There is no information about Spanish facilities in their literature. For special needs, check with your travel agent or ticket clerk.

Wheelchair reservations can be made when reservation is made.

Check-in requirements are different in each location worldwide. Always request check-in information when you make your reservation, to avoid jeopardizing your plans.

LUFTHANSA

Lufthansa is the West German airline. It carried 11,704,836 passengers in 1977 to 113 cities in 70 countries. In North America, Lufthansa serves Anchorage, Edmonton, Calgary, Winnipeg, Montreal, New York, Boston and Los Angeles. From those cities the routes penetrate every corner of the globe.

Aircraft: The Lufthansa fleet is composed of:

<pre>
 6 Boeing 747
30 Boeing 727
30 Boeing 737
11 McDonnell Douglas DC-10
 5 Airbus 300
</pre>

Special services: Lufthansa offers its passengers special services, including special meals and certain medical accommodations. In addition, Lufthansa has the best discount rates for tours of Germany.

Executive Traveler Service is Lufthansa's name for its business travelers' special plan. It offers the following services:

Hotel reservations at Intercontinental hotels can be made through Lufthansa with immediate confirmation.

Conference rooms are available at airports wherever Lufthansa lands. Five days' advance notice is required.

A bilingual secretary is available with five days' advance notice.

Executive Mail Service will have your mail sent to Lufthansa offices around the world. Mail is held until you pick it up.

Business cards can be printed in a foreign language. Five days' notice required.

The timetable is a very readable, informative publication and has information about connecting and check-in times at all airports served by Lufthansa, and that's a lot!

Meals are provided for those passengers with dietary, religious, health or personal needs if requested when the reservation is made.

Handicapped services and provisions are standard. All arrangements will be taken care of if enough notice is given. Contact your travel agent or ticket clerk to make arrangements. The Lufthansa headquarters in Frankfurt, West Germany, is well designed to attend to handicapped needs.

Wheelchair reservations are taken at same time as ticket reservations. Remember that exotic destinations may not be equipped to deal with your needs. Give Lufthansa ample time to set up arrangements.

Check-in requirements vary worldwide. Lufthansa's timetable has a very useful chart that gives *both* check-in time requirements *and* time required to transfer from an incoming plane to an outgoing domestic or international flight for a large number of cities. Check this timetable, but always get your information from airline personnel to be certain it's up-to-date.

JAPAN AIR LINES

Japan Air Lines serves the U.S. from New York with connecting West Coast locations. There are no Europe-bound flights from the U.S. on JAL. Their service extends to all parts of the Orient and the Pacific and then continues westbound to Europe, India, Russia and Egypt. In 1977, 9,925,920 passengers flew JAL.

Aircraft: The JAL fleet is composed of:

27 Boeing 747
 6 McDonnell Douglas DC-10
41 McDonnell Douglas DC-8
 2 Boeing 727

Special services: JAL provides special services for its passengers. The most common of these are special meals and certain medical accommodations. In addition JAL provides promotional plans that make it distinct from the other airlines.

JAL's timetable gives at least partial timetables for the following airlines that it connects with in Asia: Japan Asia

Airways, Cathay Pacific, Singapore Airlines, Philippine Airways, Qantas, Air India, Malaysian Airline System, Garuda Indonesian Airways. If you need information about these lines contact JAL.

Brochures, guides and explicit outlines of business, social and cultural customs in the Orient, *plus* very helpful books outlining services, hotels and theaters in all major Japanese cities are available on request.

Meals are provided for all passengers who have special dietary, religious, health or personal needs, if requested at time reservation is made.

Handicapped services and provisions are standard. Any special boarding, in-flight or airport services that may be required should be arranged well in advance of flight. Contact your travel agent or JAL ticket clerk for information.

Wheelchair reservations are available in major metropolitan areas if requested when ticket is reserved. For smaller Asian airports, make special inquiries.

Note: The much troubled and controversial new Tokyo airport is open. Information on facilities is available. One important fact: Make sure you leave at least 5 hours between your arrival at Narita Airport (the new airport—used for all international flights) and any transfer you might be making to Haneda Airport (the old airport—used for domestic Japanese flights). Narita is located 40 miles outside of Tokyo. (Taxi rides from Narita to downtown Tokyo cost the equivalent of $50!)

Check-in requirements vary throughout the world. For JAL regulations, check with the airline for each point of boarding to avoid needlessly jeopardizing your reservation.

AIR FRANCE

Air France was founded in 1933 by the merger of several small European-based international airlines. Air France began with a pioneering London–Paris route and today travels an international network that covers 357,000 miles of air routes, touching 152 cities in 75 countries. From

London to Los Angeles and Denmark to Dar es Salaam, few airlines cover the globe like Air France. In 1976 it transported 9,324,626 passengers.

Aircraft: The Air France fleet is composed of:

  4 Concorde Supersonic
18 Boeing 747
10 Boeing 707
20 Boeing 727
  2 Boeing 737
23 Caravelle
  7 Airbus A 300B2
  4 Airbus A 300B4

Special services: Air France has traditionally relied on its style and service. Now with the Concorde on one hand and charter packages on the other, it hopes to cover all aspects of air travel.

The Concorde is the most special and the most controversial of all AF features. This new supersonic transport is as much a financial burden on the French as on the English. But it lumbers along at the amazing speed of 1350+ m.p.h.! Other specifics include: Cost—$862 one way New York-Paris; service—elegant continental feasting; seating—holds 100 passengers.

Air France has a series of very helpful brochures for the tourist and the business traveler. Ask for the information you need.

Meals are provided for those passengers who have special dietary, religious, health or personal needs if requested at the time you make your reservation. Regular meals are supposed to be high-quality French food.

Handicapped services and provisions are standard in the air. The French airports around Paris have detailed provisions for the handicapped. Any in-flight needs should be arranged well ahead of departure.

Wheelchair reservations are available if made ahead of time. For exotic locales make special inquiries well ahead of time.

Check-in requirements are different in each location worldwide. Get specific information from your travel agent or airline clerk when you make your reservations so that you don't needlessly jeopardize your reservations.

SCANDINAVIAN AIRLINES SYSTEM

SAS, the Danish-based Scandinavian airline, flies to every corner of the globe. Its North American service includes New York, Chicago, Los Angeles, Seattle, Anchorage, Montreal. From those cities, SAS flies to all of Europe, 6 African countries, Asia and 5 South American locales—a total of 98 cities in 50 countries. SAS is known for good service and performance. It offers very useful information to Scandinavian-bound travelers and some special travel packages to all of their 7,469,000 passengers.

Aircraft: The SAS fleet is composed of:

    3 Boeing 747
    3 Boeing 727
    5 McDonnell Douglas DC-10
   11 McDonnell Douglas DC-8
   54 McDonnell Douglas DC-9

Special services: SAS provides special services for its passengers. Special meals and certain medical facilities are the most common. In addition, SAS has its own promotional plans that make it distinct from the others.

Family fares are available on economy/coach flight within Scandinavia and to Europe on most SAS flights. Head of family pays full regular or special fare and accompanying family members fly for 50 percent! Ask your travel agent or SAS ticket clerk to make arrangements for your intra-European flights before you go.

Business persons' discounts are available to full-fare travelers going to Copenhagen. Ask your travel agent about hotel discounts, conference-room rentals and reduced rates on translator services, etc. All such plans must be made at time of ticket reservation.

Brochures on Scandinavia are plentiful and very detailed. Ask for *Low-Cost Vacationing in Scandinavia* and *Getting Around Overseas*. These will offer you invaluable tips on the best buys available.

Meals are provided to passengers with dietary, religious, health or personal needs if requested at least 24 hours before departure. The SAS offering is extensive. Ask for their special menu that explains what is available. Also request information about their fish menu, a unique feature.

Handicapped services and provisions are available with prior notice. Any passengers who cannot be seated in regular seats can also be transported if plans are made when the ticket reservation is secured.

Wheelchair reservations can be made at the time you make your ticket reservation. For exotic destinations, leave enough time for plans to be confirmed.

Check-in requirements are varied from airport to airport and country to country. Always check with your ticket agent at the time you make your reservations to avoid jeopardizing your reservation.

ALITALIA

Italy's airline, Alitalia, departs from Philadelphia, New York and Boston in the U.S. and Montreal and Toronto in Canada to 100 cities in 60 countries in Europe, Africa, Southeast Asia and South America. Alitalia carried 6.5 million passengers in 1977.

Aircraft: The Alitalia fleet is composed of:

    5 Boeing 747
    8 McDonnell Douglas DC-10-30
    8 McDonnell Douglas DC-8-62
    7 Boeing 727-200
  33 McDonnell Douglas DC-9 and
    9 Stretch

Special services: Alitalia provides certain special services to its customers. Special meals and certain medical accommodations are the most common. In addition, Alitalia has special promotional plans that set it apart from its competition. Alitalia, being Italy's only international airline, specializes on tours of that country. They are particularly good on short-term stopovers in the major cities.

Meals for those passengers with special dietary, religious, health or personal needs are available if requested at time of ticket reservation.

Handicapped services and provisions are standard. Although no mention of these procedures is made in any Alitalia literature, they will provide the necessary facilities whenever possible.

Wheelchair reservations can be made at time of ticket reservation.

Check-in requirements vary worldwide. Always get check-in information when you make your reservations to avoid jeopardizing your ticket.

KLM—ROYAL DUTCH AIRLINES

KLM, the Royal Dutch Airline, is the oldest airline in continuous operation. It is particularly well run, offering a wide range of charters, tours, special discounts and interesting suggestions for the Europe-bound traveler. Its route is global, taking it from Miami, Chicago, Houston, New York, Montreal, Toronto, Vancouver, Calgary, Edmonton and the Caribbean to 115 cities in 70 countries. KLM carried 4.4 million passengers on its 227,720 miles of routes in 1977.

Aircraft: The KLM fleet is composed of:

8 Boeing 747
6 McDonnell Douglas DC-10
18 McDonnell Douglas DC-9
16 McDonnell Douglas DC-8

Special services: KLM provides its passengers with special services. The most common are special meals and certain medical accommodations. In addition, KLM has its own promotional plans that make it distinct from the others. KLM is particularly full of bargain tours, discount land packages, tourist incentives, etc.

Triple F Economy Class is the name KLM gives to its full-fare coach plan. For passengers who have paid the full price of a coach ticket, it offers faster airport check-ins at a special counter, seat reservations in a section separated from the rest of the plane, speedy transfers and fast luggage claim at your destination. The seats are limited, so contact your travel agent or ticket clerk early to make reservations.

JFK Airport: The KLM passenger terminal area in New York has shower and locker room facilities for the travel-weary passenger who needs to freshen up upon arrival.

Brochures are very informative, not only about Holland but about all of Europe. Ask for a copy of *Handy Facts for Travelers, The Worldwide Hotel Guide, Budget Travel Tips, Seeing Europe by Car, Surprising Amsterdam,* and their *Guide to the Dutch Caribbean.*

Meals for passengers with special dietary, religious, health or personal needs are available if requested at time of reservation.

Handicapped services and provisions are available upon request. Always contact your travel agent or ticket clerk early so that special seating, boarding and in-flight services can be arranged. Schiphol, the new airport in Amsterdam, is well equipped to deal with any of the handicapped travelers' needs.

Wheelchair reservations should be made when ticket reservation is secured.

Check-in requirements vary world-wide. Always get check-in information when you make your reservations.

INDEPENDENT AIRLINES

IATA (International Air Transport Association) is a very powerful international airline organization. Some airlines do not belong to IATA, however, and are free to set their own fares. Laker and Icelandic are leaders in transatlantic flights at a discount.

LAKER

The gadfly of international travel, Freddie Laker has created a one-man revolution in air travel. First he began with low-priced charter flights, advanced payment plans and the like. Now he has introduced the budget and standby fares for transatlantic travel. Things may never be the same.

Laker flies a McDonnell Douglas DC-10 and Boeing 707 on its transatlantic flights. Service is from London's Gatwick, Manchester and Prestwick airports to New York's Kennedy.

LAKER ABCs (ADVANCE BOOKING CHARTERS)

Purchase—final payment is due 21 days prior to scheduled departure.

Application: ABCs are available between Los Angeles and San Francisco and London, and between New York's Kennedy airport and London.

Validity: Round-trip tickets can be purchased from one week to six months prior to departure.

Savings: Peak prices run about $360 round trip. This is less than half the regular coach fare.

LAKER SKYTRAIN SERVICE

This is Laker's no-waiting, mass-market air service.

Purchase: In New York buy your ticket the same day as your flight, anytime between 4:00 A.M. and 9:30 P.M., at the Laker Travel Center, 95–25 Queens Boulevard, Rego Park, Queens, New York, Entrance on Junction Boulevard. Between 6:30 A.M. and 7:30 P.M. tickets can be purchased at 1 East 59th Street and in the lobby of One World Trade Center in Manhattan. Baggage check-in is still done in Rego Park in Queens. There are shuttle busses to JFK.

In Los Angeles, buy your ticket in the L.A. International Airport from 4:00 A.M. on.

Only one-way tickets are sold. Return tickets must be purchased in London. One person may buy two tickets or one family member may buy the whole family's tickets, as long as he has the passports and baggage for all the passengers.

Food service is purchased at that time. Breakfast is $3, cold dinner is $3, coffee and tea are 25 cents, movie and music are $2.

Application: Skytrain is available between New York and London and between Los Angeles and London.

Savings: The fare, round trip from New York, is $250 subject to the exchange rate and inflation. This savings is 66 percent off regular coach fares. From Los Angeles, it is $433 round trip during peak season.

ICELANDIC

The oldest, most-established transatlantic independent airline is Icelandic. It flies from Chicago and New York to Iceland and Luxembourg. All of Icelandic's personnel are trained in the U.S. Its aircraft—McDonnell Douglas DC8s—all meet the highest international standards.

All Icelandic flights round-trip New York to Luxembourg cost $299 plus $3 tax. This fare requires no pre-payment and is available anytime.

CARIBBEAN AND SOUTH AMERICA

There are many small airlines that serve the southern hemisphere. Below is a country by country list of some of the airlines. Check their rates and special promotional tours if you are heading south. They can offer you a great deal on air and land packages.

Brazil—Varig Airlines: Varig flies Boeing 707s and DC-10s from New York, Miami and Los Angeles to all of South America.

Venezuela—VIASA Airlines: VIASA flies out of Boston, New York and Miami to Caracas. It uses DC-8s for this route.

Ecuador—Ecuatoriana Airlines: Departing from the Aer Lingus terminal in Kennedy International Airport, this airline flies to Chile, Peru, Ecuador and Colombia.

Peru—AeroPeru: From Miami and Los Angeles, they fly to many South American cities. They use both Boeing 747s and DC-8s.

Chile—Lan Chile: Departing from Kennedy Airport in New York and Miami, Lan flies Boeing 707s and 727s to South America. Of special interest is their Easter Island tour offering.

San Salvador—TACA: This airline flies from Miami and New Orleans to San Salvador.

Jamaica—Air Jamaica: Their Boeing 727s and DC-8 and 9s fly out of New York, Miami, Philadelphia and Toronto and all over the Caribbean area.

Trinidad and Tobago—B.W.I.A.: A thriving airline, it flies Boeing 707s and DC-9s out of New York, Montreal and Miami to London and the Caribbean.

CHAPTER SEVEN
AIRPORTS OF THE WORLD

In this chapter we take you around the world, from Los Angeles to Rome, to let you see how the major airports of the world are run. Most airports provide certain basic services to passengers—restaurants, shops, first aid, currency exchanges and banks, car rental, transportation to nearby cities, and even hotels. The exact nature of these provisions plus any special features or defects and the layout of check-in counters and boarding gates are all clearly explained.

Specific costs given for transportation or services may change without notice. The figures given here are only a guideline to let you know the least you can expect to be charged. One word of advice: ask—that's right, *ask* the cost of all cab rides, parking charges or the like before you find yourself trapped in a costly situation.

THE WORLD'S WORST AIRPORTS:

This is not a very nice distinction for an airport to have. An important annual survey conducted by the Airline Pilots Association exposes the facilities its member pilots feel are most in need of improvement. The hope is that public exposure will force the airports to improve their operations.

We reprint the 1977–78 APA survey but note that the APA asked us to make it clear that the incidence of accidents is not necessarily higher at such airports. The horrible on-ground collision in Tenerife in 1976 did not occur at a badly rated facility. Conversely, certain airports on the APA list have not had a serious accident in years. This may prove that the pilots are truly masters of bad situations! They are simply asking for a little help from the ground. Therefore, what the list does indicate is the locations where the pilots feel they are operating under the most strain.

THE RATING SYSTEM

Black Star—critically deficient
Red Star—seriously deficient
Orange Star—deficient

The APA rated 22 airports with a black star; 236 with a red star and 258 with orange.

U.S. BLACK STAR AIRPORTS

- Los Angeles International Airport
LAX receives this rating because nighttime noise abatement regulations make it necessary to follow inflexible approach routes into and out of the airport. The pilots say this contradicts a basic tenet of airplane safety. The problem of noise abatement regulations is not only Los Angeles's problem. All large metropolitan airports face it because they were not designed with consideration to this problem. What is needed is redesign or relocation, and both of those alternatives are unthinkably expensive. There does not seem a satisfactory alternative at present. Only retrofitted or newly designed quiet jet engines will find both sides satisfied. Until then, hold your ears or hold your breath!

- Truman Airport—Saint Thomas, Virgin Islands.
This airport suffers badly from runways that are *too short* for the new jet aircraft. This means that the pilots must use the 100-foot soft lip at the end of the runway for extra taxiing room, so they can get up enough speed

to get off the ground and over the surrounding mountains. *Renovations have been promised.* Until then, travel light! That's what the airlines do.

Takeoffs are made with minimal amounts of fuel so the plane will be light as possible. A refueling stop is made immediately on another Virgin Island for the flight home.

- Pago Pago International, American Samoa
  This airport has a black star because of its poor runway conditions, inadequate landing aids, taxiways, radio communications and weather reporting procedures.

Other international airports with a black star rating are in the following locations:

- Australia: Kalgoorlie, Learmonth and Meekatharra;
- Colombia, South America: Barranquilla, Bogota, Cali, Cartagena, Leticia, Medellin and San Andres Island;
- Fiji: Suva;
- Greece: Corfu;
- Indonesia: Ujung Pandang;
- Italy: Rimini;
- Solomon Islands: Honiara;
- Tonga: Tongatapu;
- Venezuela: Caracas, Maturin; and
- Western Samoa: Apia.

U.S. RED STAR AIRPORTS

- Anchorage, Alaska
  This airport is given a red star because there is no cross wind runway. Construction is now underway, and they expect the star will be removed when the work is done.
- Honolulu Airport, Hawaii
  Here the absence of grooving in the runway surface (which can provide drainage of water from the runways, so the aircraft have a drier surface against which they can break their speed), lack of runway landing lights and bad control tower procedures make this a red star airport.

U.S. AIRPORTS

The major airports or "large hubs" in the U.S. account for more than 67 percent of all air passenger traffic. In 1977 over 240 million passengers boarded scheduled U.S. airlines.

O'HARE INTERNATIONAL

O'Hare is the country's busiest airport. More than 18 million domestic and one million international passengers flew out of O'Hare in 1977. They were carried on 640,000 flights!

Location: O'Hare is located 18 miles northwest of downtown Chicago, near several expressways, and served by an extensive system of public and private transportation.

Transportation facilities: Public transportation is provided by the CTA (Chicago Transit Authority) bus service 24 hours a day.

O'Hare Express Bus #40 stops in front of each terminal every 15 minutes during peak periods. The CTA provides express service between the airport and the Jefferson Park Transit Center, where many connections with bus and rapid transit lines are made. The cost is 75 cents one way. General information about all bus routes and schedules is available from the CTA (312) 670-5000.

Private automobiles: Cars travel to O'Hare via the Kennedy expressway, Tri-State or Northwest tollways. Loading and unloading of passengers is permitted by the curb in front of each terminal on both upper and lower levels. Parking is abundant—14,000 parking spaces are available. In addition to three outdoor lots, there is an enclosed, six-level garage adjacent to all three terminals and connected to them by five underground walkways. The cost is the same in the garage as in the outside lots regardless of the length of stay. The rates are approximately 65 cents an hour for the first four hours (or fraction thereof) with a maximum of $3.50 a day. Shuttle buses provide transportation from the outlying lots to the terminal.

Taxi service: Chicago taxis can take you within the city limits and to suburban locations. Suburban taxis may not operate within the city of Chicago.

To obtain a taxi at the domestic terminal, see an attendant at the dispatch booth in front of each terminal. At the international terminal, use the phone located on the outside wall of the terminal, facing the roadway. The cost from the airport to downtown is about $10. Suburban destination charges are often calculated as the meter reading plus return trip or else a flat prearranged rate. For unmetered trips get the fare before your trip begins!

Private limo services: At each domestic terminal and at the end of the international terminal, prereserved limo pickups are made. The Chicago Yellow Pages, your travel agent or airlines will give you information about how to make such a reservation.

Airport bus service: Continental Air Transport provides bus connections between the major Chicago hotels and the airport. For general information call 454-7800. The cost one way is $3.50. The pickup area is on the lower level roadway outside of each terminal building.

Out-of-town-bus services: There are many different bus and limo lines that provide transportation to Wisconsin, Indiana and southern Illinois locations. They all stop at the lower level roadway outside the terminals.

For information, contact: Hammond, Yellow and Checker Cab 768-8686 for transportation to Gary and Hammond, Indiana, and Lansing, Illinois. Phone O'Hare Wisconsin Limousine Service 427-3103 for transportation to northern Illinois and southern Wisconsin. Tri-State Coach Lines 374-7200 serves south Chicago suburbs and northwest Indiana.

Hotel pickup services: Hotels and motels have bus/limo pickup points at both ends of the domestic terminal and in front of the international terminal. Check with your hotel when you make your reservations to see if they offer this service.

Hotel facilities: The O'Hare Hilton is right across from the central terminal. To make reservations, contact your travel agent or call the Hilton nearest you. Adjacent to the airport, along the expressways, are many other hotel/motel facilities, many of which can be called direct from the airport courtesy phones.

Airport facilities and services: O'Hare is a vast complex. Its terminal is particularly spread out and hard to negotiate. So put on your walking shoes and take out your map. You are about to enter O'Hare! From one end of the airport to the other, it's about a 12-minute walk!

There is a wide range of shops and services in the airport. In the international wing, terminal one, are all the boarding ticket counters and boarding gates for international arrivals, plus customs, a currency exchange, newsstand, restaurant/bar and flight insurance booth.

On the upper level of the domestic wing in terminals two and three are ticket counters and boarding gates for domestic flights, plus gift shops, information booth, newsstand, candy store, restaurants, bars, coffee shops, telephones, USO, barbershop/shoe repair, first aid and pharmacy.

On the lower level are the baggage claim areas, ground transportation facilities, car rental counters and hotel courtesy phones.

Handicapped facilities are extensive: Elevator service from parking garages to terminal levels, and a moving sidewalk from the garage underground to the terminals provide access. Bathrooms, telephones, lounges, lockers and walkways all have been built to accommodate wheelchair access. Registered nurses are available 24 hours a day to assist wheelchair-confined passengers with any personal or hygienic services. The nurses' stations are located in the upper level of terminals two and three.

Handicapped parking: Two hundred extra-wide parking spaces are available in the elevated parking garage. There is easy access to the airport from these spots.

Medical facilities and first-aid stations in the upper levels of terminals two and three provide registered nurses and offer private facilities for mothers to feed or change their babies.

General information is available from information booths on the upper level of terminals two and three. Bilingual receptionists are there from 9:00 A.M. to 9:00 P.M. to assist any traveler. In the international terminal a multilingual staff is available in the federal inspection area.

Emergency assistance can be received by phone. Police can be summoned by calling 686-2230; first aid, 686-2288 or 2289; multilingual receptionists, 686-2304; pharmacy, 686-7411; Allright Auto Parks operator, 686-7525; parking complaints, 686-2321.

Airlines that serve O'Hare. The following airlines all fly into and out of O'Hare:

Scheduled Airlines

Aer Lingus	KLM
Air Canada	Lufthansa
Air France	Mexicana
Air Jamaica	North Central
Allegheny	Northwest Orient
American	Ozark
Braniff	Piedmont
British Airways	SAS
Continental	Southern
Delta	Swissair
Eastern	TWA
Frontier	United
Icelandic	

Commuter Airlines

Air Wisconsin	Mississippi Valley
Britt Airways	Phillips
Midstate Airlines	Seaco

Supplemental Carriers

Capitol	TIA
ONA	World

ATLANTA INTERNATIONAL AIRPORT
HARTSFIELD AIRPORT

Surprisingly, Atlanta is the second busiest airport in the U.S. More than 14,970,115 passengers flew out of this facility in 1977. Atlanta is important as a hub because it serves as a central connecting station for flights from the East Coast, the South and the Caribbean.

Location: Hartsfield is located just eight miles southwest of Atlanta, off Interstate 85. The travel time varies with traffic. Allow 30 minutes at least.

Transportation facilities: Unlike many older metropolitan airports, Atlanta does not have any public transportation links between downtown and the airport.

Private automobiles: Cars are the simplest way to reach the airport from downtown. Parking is ample. Long-term remote parking is $2 a day. In the west lot it is $3 a day; in the central lot it is $6 a day. Short-term parking in the deck lot near the terminal is 50 cents for the first half hour.

Taxi service: is available if you call. Limos are more convenient.

Limo service: Downtown hotels are pickup points for limos. Cost: $3.50.

Airport facilities and services: There is a wide range of shops and facilities available in Atlanta's airport.

The first level contains hotel phones, baggage claim and car rentals. The mezzanine has dining rooms and cocktail lounges. The main level, west wing, contains traveler's aid, snack bar, cafeteria, newsstand, shoe shine, pharmacy, country food store and insurance booths. The main level, east wing, has a toy shop, gift and clothing shops, bank, flower cart, lost and found, a food shop, barbershop, first aid and traveler's aid rooms.

Hotel facilities: There are nine hotel/motels in the immediate area of the airport. Over 2,300 rooms are available. All major chains are represented. Downtown Atlanta is not far, and your travel agent can give you a complete listing of all Atlanta hotels.

Handicapped facilities: Special restrooms, telephone booth and unlimited access to all airport areas are provided for those in wheelchairs. Medical attention is available from the first-aid station on the main floor behind Southern Airlines' ticket counter.

Medical facilities: First-aid stations are staffed by nurses who can treat minor needs. Major medical problems are referred to Atlanta hospitals. Contact any airport employee in an emergency situation, and he or she will arrange for an ambulance and attendants.

Traveler's Aid: An office in Hartsfield is provided to give advice and help to destitute or stranded travelers. It is located next to the first-aid station.

Airlines that serve Hartsfield: The following airlines all fly in and out of Hartsfield.

Scheduled Airlines

Delta	Piedmont
Eastern	Southern
National	TWA
Northwest	United

Commuter Airlines

Air South	Southeastern
Florida	Trans Air Express

LOS ANGELES INTERNATIONAL

With 10,870,000 passengers enplaned in 1977 and with more than 144,608 individual aircraft takeoffs, L.A. International Airport is the third busiest airport in the U.S. and the world.

Location: The L.A. airport is situated 18 miles southwest of downtown L.A. on the Pacific coast.

Transportation facilities: The freeway is the key to getting anywhere in L.A., including the airport. There are several bus lines, limos, and taxis to choose from if you don't go by car.

Private automobiles: Cars are advised to allow at least two hours' driving time to get to the airport on holidays, during rush hours or in the summer. The distances are not so great but the traffic is murder! Up-to-date traffic conditions are given on the radio and you should listen to them. As you near the airport, tune to 530 on your AM dial for airport traffic and parking information.

Parking is abundant. In the short-term lot, it is 50 cents each two hours. In the central lot, it is $6 a day. There are three long-term lots. In lot A, it is 50 cents each two hours, $4 a day; in lot C, it is 50 cents each three hours, $2 a day; in the VSP lot, it is 50 cents for the first six hours, $1.50 a day.

Free tram service connects lots to terminals.

Taxi service: Service is available from the front of all terminals to all points. Sample costs are $14 to downtown Los Angeles, $13 to Beverly Hills, and $9 to Santa Monica.

Private limo services: Check with your travel agent or the L.A. telephone book for information. For additional information, see bus services listed below.

Airport bus services: Because of the enormous geographical area that L.A. Airport serves, there are seven bus lines connecting it with all of greater Los Angeles. The L.A. city buses (RTD) cost 45 cents plus 10 cents for transfers; 80 cents for freeway. Exact change is necessary. For information 24 hours a day, call 973-1222 or 626-4455.

RTD Airport Express buses, 626-4455 or 973-1222, go to downtown L.A., Hollywood, Wilshire, Beverly Hills and Universal City for $3.50. To Ontario airport it is $6. They are available at bus shelters outside all terminals. Tickets are purchased from the driver with *exact change* or from ticket booths across from the baggage claim areas.

Culver City buses 559-8310 run from the airport to Westchester, Culver City, Santa Monica and West Los Angeles for 35 cents. Get more information from the ticket booths across from the baggage claim areas.

Buses for Orange County, Disneyland, Long Beach, Pasadena and nearby cities stop in front of the baggage claim areas. Tickets cost $3 to $7.50. For information 24 hours a day, call 796-9108.

The Antelope Valley bus to Newhall ($3), Palmdale ($5.50), and Lancaster ($6) departs every evening. Information and tickets can be obtained at the booth in front of the baggage claim areas (except at West Imperial Terminal) or from the bus driver. For information call 948-8421.

Crown Airport Commuter provides several trips daily to Glendale, Burbank, Hollywood, Sherman Oaks, etc. The cost is around $4. Tickets can be purchased across from baggage claim areas. For information call 641-4052.

FlyAway Bus Service to Van Nuys connects passengers to San Fernando Valley cities. $3 one way; $5 round trip. For information call 994-5554 or 781-5554.

Hotel pickup service: Free transportation to and from major L.A. area hotels is provided by buses at the tram stops outside the terminals. Ask your travel agent or hotel if they provide this service when you make your hotel reservations or use courtesy telephones located in the baggage claim areas.

Hotel facilities: There are hotels and motels all around the airport and along the freeways and in the various downtown areas. If you need a room for a short stopover or for a longer stay, see your travel agent or ask your airline for information about facilities. Courtesy phones are in the baggage claim area.

The L.A. airport is constructed so that there are seven separate terminals, called satellites, that house the airline gates. These satellites are connected by an underground channel to the airlines' ticket counters, housed in separate buildings. Check-in and baggage claim, as well as hotel phones, traveler's aid, gift shop, newsstand and luggage cart rental, are in the ticketing buildings. The satellites have snack bars, restaurants, lockers, insurance machines, nursery, gift shops, postage machines and mailbox.

All seven satellites circle the airport parking facilities, in the center of which is a restaurant and bank.

Handicapped facilities are excellent. Write to the airport public relations department or, upon arrival, request a brochure entitled *Guide for the Handicapped and Elderly*. This explains all services that are offered.

Special parking lots are available with extra-wide spaces for easy movement of wheelchair passengers. Free shuttle service from your car to the terminal is in lot C. A van with hydraulic lift provides standby shuttle service. When you land at L.A., call 646-6402 for pickup at your terminal and transportation to your car.

Ramps and elevators provide access throughout all of the airport. In addition, telephone booths and restrooms are designed for handicapped and wheelchair-confined passengers.

Medical facilities are available for minor first-aid care. Any airport employee can offer assistance. Paramedics are on hand for assistance during emergencies and one of 13 near-by hospitals is easily reached by ambulance. For more information, call 646-6254.

Traveler's Aid maintains an office in each terminal. Information, emergency financial or personal assistance is provided from 7 A.M. to 10 P.M. Monday through Friday.

Airlines that serve Los Angeles International. The following airlines fly in and out of L.A.:

Scheduled Airlines

Aerolineas Argentinas	Continental
Aero Mexico	Delta
AeroPeru	Eastern
Air Canada	Ecuatoriana
Air France	Hughes Air West
Air New Zealand	Japan Air Lines
Air Panama	Korean
American	Lufthansa
Avianca	Mexicana
Braniff	National
British	Northwest
Canadian Pacific	Pan Am
China	SAS

Seaboard World
Texas International
TWA
United

UTA
Varig
Western

Charter and Supplemental Airlines

Air Manila
British Air Tours
British Caledonian
Capitol International
Condor Flugdienst
Dan Air
Finnair
KLM
Laker

Martin Air Charter
Overseas National
Pacific Western
SABENA
Trans International
Transavia
World
Yugoslav

Commuter Airlines

Air California
Baja Cortez
Golden West
LA/Bay Area Helicopter

Pacific Southwest
Sierra Pacific
Sun Aire
Swift Aire

DALLAS/FORT WORTH
INTERNATIONAL AIRPORT

This staggeringly modern and spread-out facility has become the newest big "hub" airport in the U.S., since opening its doors in January 1974. It instantly became the fourth busiest airport in 1977, when 8,400,293 passengers departed from this facility.

Location: The Dallas/Fort Worth airport is situated on 17,500 acres of land, exactly midway between the two cities, 17 miles from each.

Transportation: Unlike older metropolitan areas, public buses do not go to the airport. Use your own car, taxis, airport buses, private limos and hotel shuttles to get there.

Private automobiles: Parking facilities are adjacent to each terminal building. In the short-term lots, it is 25 cents for the first 30 minutes, $4 a day. In the long-term lots, it is

$2 a day. Airtrans, an automated transit system, provides shuttle service between the lots and the lower levels of the terminals and costs 25 cents.

Taxi-limo service: Taxis are available from Surtran Taxicabs Inc. and from private cab companies. Round-trip limo service between the airport and Fort Worth is provided by Surtran (251-1736) and costs $3.50. Pick up the limo in Fort Worth at 615 Commerce Street. Buses leave every half hour. Allow 40 minutes for the ride. Round-trip limo service between the airport and Dallas is $4. In Dallas get the limo at the terminal on the corner of the LBJ Expressway and Coit Road. Again, buses leave every half hour. Allow an hour for the ride.

Hotel facilities: The Airport Marina Hotel is located in the heart of the airport terminal complex. For reservations or information, ask your travel agent or airline. In the airport use Airtrans for access.

Airport facilities and services: This mammoth airport has four basic terminals, shaped like horseshoes, that are connected by roadways (lower level for departing passengers, upper level for arrivals). Each terminal has basically the same facilities: restaurants, bars, newsstand, duty-free shop, car rental counter, clothing and gift shops, toy shop, barbershop, insurance counter, game room, traveler's assistance center, taxi and limo service and baggage claim.

Handicapped facilities are exceptional at Dallas/Fort Worth. First-aid stations in each terminal have personnel who will assist any traveler. The airport itself is fully automated with moving sidewalks, trams and ramps. Many telephones and drinking fountains have been lowered and elevators have signage in braille. If you are making a connection in this enormous airport, have your travel agent book you on an airline that is located in the same terminal building if possible.

Medical facilities: Dallas/Fort Worth has its own medical facility with service available around the clock. For help, contact any airline or airport employee. They will summon aid.

A traveler's assistance center is open 24 hours a day, seven days a week to help indigent or temporarily stranded passengers find shelter and food.

Airlines that serve Dallas/Fort Worth. The following airlines fly in and out of Dallas/Fort Worth:

Scheduled Airlines

Air Canada	Eastern
American	Frontier
Braniff	Ozark
Continental	Texas International
Delta	

Commuter Airlines

Air Illinois	
Chaparral	Metroflight
Eagle	Rio
Great Plains	Scheduled Skyways

JOHN FITZGERALD KENNEDY INTERNATIONAL AIRPORT

JFK is the largest of the three metropolitan New York airports. Used for all international flights and any jumbo jets, it is the fifth busiest airport in the U.S. In 1977, 7,701,986 passengers boarded planes at JFK.

Location: Situated on land reclaimed from the ocean 15 miles southeast of midtown Manhattan in Queens, JFK covers nearly 5000 acres.

Transportation facilities: There are many, many methods of access to and from the airport. Private car, bus, limo, taxi, helicopter, even subway can all be used.

Private automobiles: Expressway connections from all metro areas are good. Once you arrive at the airport, there are good parking facilities. Long-term parking is $2 a day. (Shuttle service between terminals is 50 cents.) Short-term parking is 50 cents an hour on top of the Pan Am terminal in lot 6. Other short-term lots cost $6 maximum a day.

Taxi service: Taxi service to and from the airport is always available. From midtown Manhattan allow at least one hour. The minimum cost is $14.

Private limo services: For limo service from Long Island to and from JFK, contact Long Island-Airports Limousine (656-7000). The cost is $5 up, depending on the distance.

For other destinations contact your travel agent or consult the New York Yellow Pages. (Prices from Manhattan to JFK are about $35.)

Airport bus services: Carey Transportation (962-6623) provides regular bus service between Kennedy and the East Side Airlines Terminal at First Avenue and 37th Street every 20 minutes during the day and as flight schedules demand at night. The cost is $4. Allow one hour for travel time. To get the bus to Manhattan, check with bus employees outside the main terminal or at the baggage claim areas.

Connections to LaGuardia or Newark Airports: If you have a flight to catch at another New York area airport, here's what to do:

From JFK to La Guardia: A bus outside the main arrivals terminal leaves every 30 minutes except from 1:00 A.M. to 5:30 A.M., when it runs once an hour. The cost is $3. For more information, call Carey Transportation at 632-0500.

Helicopter service may be arranged through your airline. If you are making a connection on the same airline, the ride may be free! Always ask. Otherwise, have the airline make arrangements and reservations. The cost is $11–$16.

From JFK to Newark: Salem Transportation (212) 656-4511 or (201) 961-4250, provides limo service from the main arrivals terminal from 9:30 A.M. to 8:30 P.M. daily. The cost is $9.

Helicopter service may be arranged through your airline. Again, if you are making a connection on the same airline, the ride may be free. Just ask. Otherwise, have your airline make the arrangements and reservations. The cost is about $30.

Hotel pickup services: Hotels throughout the metropolitan area offer limo services to and from the airport. Ask your travel agent or hotel reservation clerk for information.

Hotel facilities: The International Hotel (995-9000) on the airport grounds has a shuttle service from the front of the various terminals to the hotel. Hotels in New York maintain courtesy phones in the baggage claim areas. Whenever possible, make reservations through a travel agent well ahead of time because rooms in midtown Manhattan are often sold out.

Airport facilities and services: There is a wide range of shops and services within each terminal at JFK. The airport is designed so that many of the airlines have their own buildings. The remaining airlines use the international arrivals terminal, situated right in the center of the airport. It has a bookstore, duty-free shops, a currency exchange, car rentals and information counter. On the grounds are Catholic, Protestant and Jewish houses of worship.

Handicapped facilities are not uniform. Because of the layout of the airport, each terminal has slightly different services. Arrange for wheelchair service ahead of time. For immediate medical attention or first aid, airline employees can help or will get you to the first-aid center in the main terminal.

Medical facilities are extensive. There is a 24-hour medical center located in building 198 at 150th Street and South Cargo Road. Call 656-5344 for information. For transportation to the clinic, ask any airline employee or call the airport police at 656-4688.

A dental office is also available. If you forgot to get that tooth pulled before you left home, go to suite 2311 on the second floor of the east wing of the international arrivals building. The hours are 9:30 A.M. to 5:30 P.M. Monday, Tuesday, Thursday and Friday, and you can make an appointment by calling 656-5426.

General information is available in many languages from the information and hotel desks at the arrivals level of the main international terminal.

Airlines that serve JFK airport. The following airlines fly in and out of Kennedy Airport:

Scheduled Airlines

Aer Lingus	Iberia
Aeroflot	Iran National
Aerolineas Argentinas	JAL
Aero Mexico	KLM
Air Afrique	Korean
Air Canada	Lan Chile
Air France	LOT-Polish
Air India	LTU
Air Jamaica	Lufthansa
Air New England	National
Air Panama	New York Airways
Alia-Royal Jordanian	Nigeria
Alitalia	Northwest
Allegheny	Olympic
American	Pakistan
Avianca	Pan Am
Braniff	Piedmont
British	Royal Air Maroc
British Caledonian	SABENA
BWIA (British West Indian)	SAS
Czechoslovak	South African
Delta	Swissair
Dominicana	Syrian Air
Eastern	TAP
Ecuatoriana	TAROM
Egyptair	Varig
El Al	Viasa
Finnair	Yugoslav

Supplemental Airlines

Aviaco	Condor
Altair	Danair
Balair	Evergreen
Capitol	Icelandic

Kar-Air
Laker
Maersk
Martinair
McCullough
Modern Air
Overseas National (ONA)

Sata
Saturn
Spantax
Trans International
 (TIA)
Transavia
World

Commuter Airlines
Air Atlantic
Albany Air Services
Catskill
Command
Commuter

Cumberland
Empire
Monmouth
Pilgrim
Suburban

LA GUARDIA AIRPORT

LaGuardia is the sixth busiest airport in the U.S. Serving as an important link between international and national traffic and as a central hub for the Northeast, LaGuardia handled more than 7,586,096 departing passengers in 1977. Each passenger paced through the 1,300 feet—from one end to another—that is LaGuardia!

Location: LaGuardia is eight road miles from midtown Manhattan. During rush hour it can seem much farther.

Transportation facilities: There is an extensive network of private cars, taxis, limos, buses and even helicopters that join LaGuardia to the surrounding metropolitan areas.

Private automobiles: There is no long-term parking lot at LaGuardia. All cars must use the new garage or the open lots and pay a lot for either one. Parking in the garage costs $7 a day; in the lot $5 a day. Short-term parking is available at meters right across from the terminal. Cost is 25 cents per 15 minutes.

Taxi service: Taxis are always available in Manhattan and at the airport. The fare to midtown is about $10.

Private limo service: Have your travel agent or airline

find out what companies serve the New York area. Consult the Yellow Pages.

Airport bus service: Carey Transportation buses leave the East Side Airlines Terminal, First Avenue at 37th street in Manhattan, for LaGuardia every 20 minutes from 6:45 A.M. to 11:50 P.M. with service during off hours, contingent on airline arrivals. The cost is $3. For information call 632-0500.

Helicopter service from LaGuardia to Manhattan is available. Flights depart once an hour from 8:15 A.M. to 2:35 P.M. The cost is approximately $25. Make reservations through your travel agent or airlines. Seating available without reservations on available basis.

Hotel pickup services: Various hotels have limo services available. Have your travel agent check and see if yours provides this service. Among those hotels with airline affiliations are the Americana (American) and the Hilton (TWA).

Hotel facilities: There is no hotel on the airport grounds. There are, however, many hotel/motels right around the airport. Courtesy phones are located near the baggage claim area for immediate room information in the metropolitan area.

Airport facilities and services: Because LaGuardia is a compact airport, it has little duplication of facilities. The upper level has the ticket counters and departure gates; the lower level contains the baggage claim area, buses, car rentals, a pharmacy, and restaurants. There is a wide range of shops and services located in the terminal. Below we have highlighted the most interesting and important features.

Handicapped facilities are provided throughout the terminal. Specially equipped restrooms, phone booths and rampways assure access to all airport areas. Any medical assistance required can be provided by airline personnel or airport police.

Medical facilities are provided through individual airlines. For major medical emergencies, contact the airport police at 476-5115 or the doctor on call 24 hours a day (476-5575). —

Airlines that serve LaGuardia Airport. The following airlines fly in and out of LAG:

Scheduled Airlines

American	Northwest
Allegheny	Ozark
Braniff	Piedmont
Delta	Southern
Eastern	TWA
National	United
North Central	New York Airways

Commuter Airlines

Catskill Airways	Command Airways
Commuter Airlines	Pilgrim Airlines

DENVER STAPLETON AIRPORT

The seventh busiest airport in the U.S., Stapleton, had 7,098,620 passengers pass through its gates in 1977.

Owned and operated by the city and county of Denver, this airport is an important link between both coasts and is the most important airport in that section of the West.

Location: Situated seven miles from downtown Denver, Stapleton can be easily reached in 20–30 minutes along city streets.

Transportation facilities: Private car, taxi and limo are the main methods of transportation available.

Private automobile: Cars may park in long or short-term parking lots. There are nearly 6,000 parking spaces. Long-term parking with free shuttle to the terminal costs 25 cents an hour and $2.50 for 24 hours. Short-term, near the terminal, costs 50 cents an hour and $4.50 for 24 hours.

Limo service: Two limo companies supply service to Denver. The cost is $2.30. Allow 30 minutes. For all other areas, call Airport Limo at 893-6464 or American Limo Service, 424-6930.

Hotel facilities: Ten or twelve motels surround the airport. Ask your travel agent for information or make your reservations from the airport.

Airport services and facilities: The Denver airport is a three-story building with all the boarding gates located along four concourses that extend from the main building. The first floor contains the baggage claim area, car rental counter, bank, postal service, traveler's aid, ground transportation and security office. The second floor, the main floor of the terminal, contains a newsstand, restaurants, gift shops, record store, candy and flower shops, clothing store, traveler's aid, billiards and game room, barbershop, all ticket counters and boarding gates. The third floor contains the nursery, observation area, military lounge and airline offices.

Handicapped facilities are available. Elevator access to all floors and ramps make wheelchairs usable. For special needs, make prior arrangements with each individual airline.

Medical facilities are provided for minor occurrences by individual airline's personnel. For an emergency, contact any airport employee or airport police.

Traveler's Aid has an office on the first floor, where emergency assistance is available to stranded, destitute or otherwise troubled travelers.

Airlines that serve Denver. The following airlines fly in and out of Denver:

Scheduled Airlines

Braniff	Ozark
Continental	Southern
Delta	Texas International
Frontier	TWA
Mexicana	United
North Central	Western

Commuter Airlines
  Air Midwest
  Aspen Airways
  Rocky Mountain Airways

SAN FRANCISCO INTERNATIONAL AIRPORT

The eighth largest airport in this country, San Francisco International had 7,013,208 passengers go through its gates in 1977. As part of the entire Bay Area system that includes Oakland and Berkeley airports, it is an important link in the country's air travel network.

Location: The airport is 15 miles south of San Francisco, near Daly City. It is served by many forms of public and private transportation.

Transportation facilities: There are many good systems available to the San Francisco air traveler.

Private automobiles: U.S. 101 runs right by the airport. For routes to this freeway, consult an area map.

Parking facilities are extensive and patrolled for security. December 1978 is the scheduled date for the opening of a new garage area, bringing parking spaces to a total of 7,000. Until that time, the airport suggests you use the economy lot (cost—$1 for eight hours, $3.50 for 24 hours) and take the free connecting shuttle to the terminal. The terminal garage, located directly across from the airport, holds 2,000 cars. The cost is 50 cents per hour. Six dollars maximum for 24 hours.

Taxi service: Taxis (876-2209) are available to and from the airport. From downtown San Francisco, the cost is $15; from Oakland, $26.

Note: Distances over 15 miles are computed at meter plus one-half. Ask your driver before you get in the cab!

Limo services: Limo service is available to all Bay areas. San Francisco-bound passengers should call Associated Limo at 824-2660. The cost is $22. For other destinations, call 877-0420.

Limo service is also available to Berkeley Airport for around $7. Reservations are recommended. Call 841-0150.

Airport bus service: The Airporter Coach Service (877-0345) operates from O'Farrell and Taylor streets in San Francisco to the airport for $1.40. Airport pickup is in front of the terminal. Daytime service is generally every 15 minutes; the night schedule varies.

Oakland is served by Continental Trailways and costs $1.55. Call Trailways for information. Otherwise, you will pay $26 to $36 for a taxi or private limousine to take you there!

Hotel facilities: There is a Hilton Hotel on the airport grounds. Reservations can be made through your travel agent or any Hilton Hotel office. Many other hotel/motels serve the immediate area.

Airport facilities and services: The San Francisco airport is divided into two terminals—the central and south. (A north terminal is under construction.) Each has two levels. In the central terminal, the lower level has the baggage claim area, airport bus stops, car rental counters, limo services, taxis, post office, medical facility and post office. The upper level has a shoe-shine parlor, bank, restaurants, newsstand, bar, florist, traveler's aid, insurance counter and passageways to boarding gates for United, National, Northwest, Delta and Hughes Airwest. A nursery, lost and found, USO and airport police are on the second floor.

In the south terminal, the lower level has the baggage claim, car rental counters, customs and immigration and taxi and limo stops. The upper level has the foreign currency exchange, a duty-free shop, restaurants and snack bars, cocktail lounges, gift shops, newsstands, sauna, nursery, barbershop, candy and flower shop, traveler's aid and boarding gates for American, Braniff, Continental, Air California, TWA, Philippine Airlines, Western, JAL, Qantas, China, Pan Am, Air Canada and Canadian Pacific.

Handicapped facilities and services are good here. Restrooms and telephone booths have been designed to accommodate persons in wheelchairs. Free parking for 72 hours is provided to handicapped persons in the lot between the south and central terminals. Cars must have special handicapped driver plates. Access to all parts of the termi- ‧ nals is provided by ramps and elevators.

Medical facilities are superior. Call 7-0444 on any white airport courtesy phone or ask any airport employee for assistance. New electric miniambulances with the latest life-saving devices are provided to give patient immediate care while being carried to local hospitals. It is the first such system in the U.S. For first aid, see any airport employee.

General information is available from operator on courtesy phone stations throughout terminals.

Traveler's Aid has offices in both terminals. Call 7-0188 on courtesy phones. It offers help for destitute, stranded or otherwise needy travelers.

Airlines that serve San Francisco International. The following airlines fly into and out of San Francisco:

Scheduled Airlines

Air Canada	National
American	Northwest
Braniff	Pan Am
China	Philippine
Continental	Qantas
Delta	TWA
Hughes Air West	United
JAL	Western

Commuter Airlines

Air California	Stol-Air
Cab Air	Swiftaire
Pacific Southwest	

WASHINGTON NATIONAL AIRPORT

Ranked ninth in the U.S., Washington National had 6,183,337 passengers leave its gates in 1977. This airport is an important link between Dulles and Baltimore–Washington airports. Many transfer passengers pass through National.

Location: National is located along the Potomac River, only four miles from Washington. It is easily reached by car, taxi or limo.

Transportation facilities: Metro rail, Metro bus, suburban bus lines, limos and taxis all help the passenger travel to metropolitan Washington destinations.

Private automobiles: Cars approach the airport on the George Washington Memorial Parkway. Parking facilities are good. Six parking areas provide space for 4,000 cars. The long-term lots are one mile from the terminal with free shuttle connections. The cost is $3 a day. The main, short-term lot is in front of the circle terminal. The cost is 50 cents each half hour, with a maximum of $6 a day. Short-term parking in the lot adjacent to the terminal costs 75 cents for the first half hour with $6 maximum a day.

Limo services: The main hotels in downtown D.C. are pickup and let-off points for limos. The cost is $2.75. This service is frequent during the day. At night the schedule varies.

Connecting transportation to Dulles or Baltimore airports: Buses are available from dispatch operators at terminal exits. To Dulles is a 50–70-minute trip. To Baltimore, a 60-minute trip. For information, call 471-9801.

Hotel facilities: Hotels are available in the adjoining areas and throughout the suburban areas. See courtesy phones in baggage claim areas for hotel information and reservations.

Airport facilities and services: Washington National airport is spread out—walking distance through the terminal is about 2,500 feet, or 10 minutes. The main terminal houses most ticket counters, gates and facilities but there is also a north terminal, a south finger and the Northwest-TWA terminal.

The main terminal has three levels. The lower level contains boarding gates for United, Allegheny, Eastern and American, a first-aid center (room 56), police, and lost and found (both in room 72). The first floor contains a post office, restaurants, snack bar, traveler's aid, car rental counters, bookstore, toy store, pharmacy, barbershop, baggage claim and ticket counters, boarding gates for some flights and access to the Northwest and TWA gates. The second floor contains a bank, buffeteria, terrace lounge and VIP lounges.

The north terminal has Piedmont, Braniff, National and Delta ticket counters, boarding gates, baggage claim, USO information desk, bar, newsstand, snack bar and car rental counters.

The Northwest and TWA terminal is located at the south end of the main terminal. It contains their check-in counters and boarding gates.

Handicapped facilities are provided by individual airlines. The airport itself offers assistance to handicapped travelers through its security and first-aid staff.

Medical facilities are available through first-aid nurses in room 56 on the lower level of the main terminal. For serious medical problems, contact any airport employee.

Traveler's Aid has an office in the center of the main terminal across from the Eastern shuttle counter. They offer assistance to stranded, destitute or otherwise troubled travelers.

Airlines that serve Washington National airport. The following airlines fly into and out of National:

Scheduled Airlines

Allegheny	National
American	Northwest
Braniff	Piedmont
Delta	TWA
Eastern	United Airlines

Commuter Airlines

Altair
Cumberland
Monmouth

BOSTON LOGAN INTERNATIONAL AIRPORT

The tenth busiest airport in the U.S., Boston's Logan saw 5,657,235 passengers depart from its gates in 1977. Within easy range of downtown Boston, Logan is used by the entire Northeastern U.S. as a central connecting station.

Location: Situated a short three miles from Boston, Logan is right on the Atlantic Coast.

Transportation services: There are many different ways to get to and from Logan. In addition to convenient access for cars and taxis, public transportation and bus services are abundant in the entire metropolitan area.

Private automobiles: Easily reached by expressway from downtown and suburban areas, there is parking for 10,000 cars. Three outdoor lots adjacent to each terminal and one indoor garage all cost the same: 75 cents for the first hour, $4.50 for the first 24 hours, $2.25 for each additional 12 hours.

Taxi service: Although taxis are available from the airport to downtown or suburban locations, you should always ask the price before you get in the cab, particularly if your destination is outside city limits. (Average cost from Logan to downtown Boston is $5.)

Limo services: All downtown hotels are pickup and drop-off points for the airport limo service, Airways Transportation Service, 267-4907. From them you can pick up public transportation, trains or buses to get to other localities. The cost is $3, and it takes at least 30 minutes for the trip.

Public transportation: There is an MBTA subway stop at the airport. To get to it, take the Massport interterminal shuttle bus that stops at all terminals every six to 12 minutes. The cost is 45 cents. Additional information about transportation services can be obtained at each terminal or by calling Massport operations at 567-5400.

Hotel facilities: The Logan Hilton Hotel is on the airport grounds and is accessible by the airport shuttle bus. In addition there are hotel/motel facilities throughout the downtown area. See your travel agent for advanced information or reservations. In the airport look for the courtesy information centers for hotel information.

Airport facilities and services: Logan International has four terminals: international, north, south and southwest.

The international terminal area contains foreign airlines' ticket counters and boarding gates, customs, duty-free shop, currency exchange, restaurants, traveler's aid and car rental counters. There is a parking lot adjacent to this terminal, and the Logan Hilton is just a short distance away.

The north terminal has car rental counters, bars and restaurants, a gift shop, newsstand, medical station, ticket counters, boarding gates and baggage claim area for United, Delta, TWA, North Central, Air Canada and Air New England, small commuter lines and charter lines.

The south terminal area contains ticket counters and boarding gates for National, American, Northwest, Allegheny and commuter airlines, plus restaurants, a newsstand and car rental counters.

The southwest terminal area contains check-in counters and boarding gates for Eastern and Northwest's flights, plus car rental counters, gift shops, restaurant, coffee shop, bar and newsstand.

Handicapped facilities: Logan's facilities for the handicapped include ramps, elevators, restrooms, modified telephone booths, food service tables and preferred parking at most locations. For handicapped passengers making connecting flights at Logan, special arrangements for transportation should be made ahead of time. Call 567-8010.

Medical facilities are available at the medical station located in the administration building between the north and south terminals. For emergency attention, call 726-3570, or state police at 567-2233.

Traveler's Aid maintains an office in the international terminal. Any passenger needing assistance because of lack of funds, rooms or loss of luggage should seek their help. The office is open from noon to 7:00 P.M. seven days a week.

Airlines that serve Logan International. The following airlines fly in and out of Logan Airport:

Scheduled Airlines

Aer Lingus	Air New England
Air Canada	Alitalia

Allegheny	North Central
American	Northwest
British Airways	Pan Am
Delta	Swissair
Eastern	TAP
Lufthansa	TWA
National	United

Commuter Air Carriers

Bar Harbor	Merrimack
Command	Monmouth
Commuter	Northeast
Cumberland	Pilgrim
Downeast	Precision Valley
Empire	Provincetown-Boston
Hyannis	Winnipesaukee

Nonscheduled Charter Airlines

Evergreen	Overseas National
Trans International	World Airways

FOREIGN AIRPORTS

In this section, London's two airports—Heathrow and Gatwick; Paris's two airports—Orly and DeGaulle; plus DaVinci in Rome and Frankfurt International in Germany are highlighted.

Wherever you go, from London to Lagos, it is helpful to know what to expect when you arrive at your destination. If you are traveling to any airports not covered in this chapter, we recommend that you ask your airline or the national tourist board for any airport information they have.

FRANKFURT INTERNATIONAL AIRPORT

Frankfurt Airport is one of the ten busiest airports in the world. Because it is centrally located on the European continent, it serves as an important link between the East and West.

Location: Situated 20 miles east of downtown Frankfurt, the airport is easily reached by many means of transportation within 15 to 20 minutes.

Transportation facilities: Not only are there facilities for easy access to Frankfurt, but connections to long-distance land links are also available.

Private automobiles: Private cars are accommodated in two large parking garages. Underground parking is in the garage directly across from the terminal building. The other garage is to the right of the domestic terminal. Both are connected to the terminal by underground walkways.

Bus service: A bus station on the arrivals level at all three terminals provides connections with bus routes to Frankfurt and all other destinations in Germany.

Train service: Rail connections from Frankfurt's main station (Hauptbahnhof) to other German cities may be made in the rail station in the basement of the international terminal. The trip to Frankfurt takes about 13 minutes and costs around two deutschmarks.

Taxi service: Taxis are stationed on the arrival level at all exits. The cost of the ride to city center is about 18 deutschmarks.

Hotel facilities: The Frankfurt Sheraton Hotel is directly across the roadway from the main terminal building. Special day rates are available for passengers wanting a room while they wait for a connecting flight. Any Sheraton Hotel or travel agent can help you make reservations.

Airport facilities and services: The Frankfurt airport is a marvel of modern conveniences and shops. Moving sidewalks get you from one end to the other, and elevator and escalators make access easy. The airport is divided into three zones or terminals. Zone A has domestic flights, Zone B, domestic and international, and Zone C, charters. In the main departure area are duty-free shops, passport control, post office, banks, snack shops, airport clinic, pharmacy, barber and beauty shops, ticket counters and boarding gates. On the arrivals level are the baggage claim areas, customs, car rental counters, bus station and restaurants. The lower levels have a pharmacy, shops, supermarket, railway station and the parking garage.

Handicapped facilities are good. Individual airlines will provide wheelchairs and special attention. The building itself is accessible by elevator and moving sidewalks on all levels.

Medical facilities are extensive. There is a dental care office on the departures floor in the main concourse. The medical clinic is staffed by nurses and paramedics and has emergency care equipment. Forgotten inoculations may be administered here in some cases.

Airlines serving Frankfurt International. The following airlines fly into and out of Frankfurt:

Aer Lingus	Flugfelag-Iceland
Aeroflot	Garuda Indonesian
Aerolineas Argentinas	Iberia
Air Afrique	Iran
Air Algerie	Iraqi
Air Canada	JAL
Air France	KLM
Air India	Kenya
Air Jamaica	Kuwait
Air Malta	Lan Chile
Alia Royal Jordanian	Libyan Arab
Alitalia	LOT
Ariana Afghan	Lufthansa
Austrian	Luxair
Avianca	Malaysian
British Airways	Malev-Hungarian
British Midland	Middle East
Bulgarian	National
Cyprus	Olympic
Czechoslovak	Pakistan
DLT German Domestic	Pan Am
Egyptair	Philippine
El Al	Qantas
Ethiopian	Royal Air Maroc
Finnair	Sabena

SAS
Saudi Arabian
Singapore
South African
Sudan
Swissair
Tarom-Romanian
Thai Airways

TAP
Tunis Air
Turk Hava Yollari
Varig
Viasa
Yugoslav
Zambia

LONDON AIRPORTS

The London metropolitan area is served by several airports. The two largest and most important international facilities are Heathrow and Gatwick. Below we give you all the information you'll need to get around these enormous complexes.

HEATHROW AIRPORT

Heathrow is the busiest international airport in the world! More than 70 different airlines carry 23 million passengers to every corner of the globe. (Although Chicago's O'Hare carries more passengers on domestic flights inside the U.S., its international traffic is minimal when compared to Heathrow's.)

The vast maze of gates, concourses, separate buildings and winding corridors make Heathrow a difficult airport to get around in. But don't despair. You will get your feet on the ground not long after you land!

Location: Heathrow is 15 miles west of central London. There are many different transportation links to the airport.

Transportation facilities: Connections to London and the entire country can be made by train, bus, subway (tube), car or taxi.

General transportation information: Call 897-6711 (London area code 01) for information on all current transportation links.

Private automobiles: Cars should approach the airport

through the tunnel from the M4 Motorway or the A4 (Bath) Road when traveling from London. Parking is available in short-term lots adjacent to each terminal and costs 15 pence an hour, £4.80 a day. The long-term parking lot is connected to the roadway and a shuttle service connects it to terminals. The cost is one pound a day.

Taxi service: Taxis are available at the front of each terminal. All trips that are less than 20 miles are charged by the meter. For trips more than 20 miles the driver may charge you *twice* what is on the meter, so set the fare with the driver *before* you get in the taxi. The average fare to central London is about 6–7 pounds.

Bus service: London transport buses 82, 105, 140, 223, 285 and express bus 1A all go to the airport. For information call 222-1234.

Green Line buses leave Heathrow for outlying areas every half hour. Information and buses are available outside the terminals. Airline buses are provided by British Airways, Pan Am and TWA. Call their ticket offices for information. The cost is one pound and the traveling time is 45 minutes.

Subway service: The shortest subway (tube) ride takes about 50 minutes to Piccadilly Circus in London. London Transport, 222-1234, will provide information. However, trains run anywhere from six to 15 times an hour and cost as low as 80 pence.

Helicopter service from British Caledonian Airways between Heathrow and Gatwick airports is available for 12 pounds. There are ten flights a day and reservations are not necessary.

Hotel facilities: There are 19 hotels within a four-mile radius of the airport. Free car service from the airport to hotels is provided. See the reservations desk in each terminal for any hotels in Great Britain. For reservations from Terminal 1, call 759-2710; Terminal 2, 897-0821; Terminal 3, 897-0507.

Airport facilities and services: Heathrow is an enormous complex made up of three basic terminals and a general service building (the Queen's Building) plus extensive parking and transportation facilities. The buildings are connected by underground walkways and shuttle buses.

Terminal 1 is for British and European flights operated by British and Irish airlines. The ground floor contains all arrivals facilities, including baggage claim, customs, car rental counters, hotel and rail information, a bank, the shuttle to other terminals, plus buses, taxis, limos and hotel courtesy cars. The first floor is the departure area and has check-in counters, restaurants, bars and shops for both domestic and international flights. In the international departure area are immigration and a duty-free shop.

Terminal 2 contains European flights operated by foreign (non-British) carriers. On the ground floor are the check-in counters. The first floor, or main level, has both arrivals and departures facilities, including customs, immigration, ground transportation and hotel information desks, a duty-free shop, post office, nursery, pharmacy, bank, bar, cafeteria, car rental counters. The second floor has a coffee shop, grill and bar.

Terminal 3 is divided into a departure terminal and an arrival terminal and is for all intercontinental flights. In the departure terminal on the ground floor is the check-in area and ticket counters. On the first floor is immigration and the boarding gates. In the arrival terminal on the ground floor is the baggage claim area, customs, car rental counters, hotel and ground transportation information. In the first floor is immigration and public health, boarding gates, duty-free shops, bookstore, post office, gift shop and cafeteria.

Handicapped facilities and services are very well maintained at Heathrow. All terminals have ramps, elevators and special restrooms. If the airline you are flying feels that it is necessary to use an ambulance between the passenger terminal and aircraft, they may use the British Airways ambulance. It has been generally agreed that no charge will be levied for this service.

Note: Distances between points in Heathrow are great. The

airport advises you not to travel alone unless specific arrangements for a companion have been made with your airline.

Medical services are available 24 hours a day. The facility, staffed by nursing sisters, is available for all medical needs and is located in the Queen's Building. Call 7047 (8-9-) on airport phones to summon help.

Traveler's Aid is provided by the Heathrow Wel-Care. Personal emergencies and travel problems are handled from 9:00 A.M. to 7:00 P.M. Monday–Friday and 9:30 A.M. to 5:30 P.M. weekends.

Airlines serving Heathrow—The following airlines fly into and out of Heathrow:

Aer Lingus
Aerolineas Argentinas
Aeroflot
Air Algerie
Air Canada
Air Ceylon
Air France
Air India
Air Jamaica
Air Malta
Air Mauritius
Air Zaire
Alia, Royal Jordanian
  Airlines
Alitalia
Ariana-Afghan
  Airlines
Austrian Airlines
Balkan-Bulgarian
  Airlines
Bangladesh Biman
British Airways
British Midland
  Airways

British West Indian
  Airways
Brymon Airways
Cyprus Airways
Czechoslovak Airlines
East African Airways
Egyptair
El Al
Ethiopian Airlines
Finnair
Ghana Airways
Gulf Air
Iberia Airlines
Icelandair
Iranair
Iraqi Airways
Japan Air Lines
Jugoslav Airlines
KLM Royal Dutch
  Airlines
Kuwait Airways
Libyan Arab Airlines
Loftleidir Icelandic
  Airlines

LOT Polish Airlines
Lufthansa German
  Airlines
Luxair
Malaysian Airlines
  System
Malev Hungarian
  Airlines
Middle East Airlines
National Airlines
Nigeria Airways
Olympic Airways
Pan American World
  Airways
PIA Pakistan International
  Airline
QANTAS
Royal Air Maroc
Sabena, Belgian Airlines

Saudi-Arabian Airlines
SAS Scandinavian Airlines
  System
Singapore Airlines
South African Airways
Sudan Airways
Swissair
Syrian Arab Airlines
TAP Portuguese Airways
TAROM—Romanian
  Airlines
Thai International
Trans World Airlines
Tunis Air
Turkish Airlines
Varig—Brazilian Airlines
VIASA—Venezuelan
  Airlines
Zambia Airways

GATWICK AIRPORT

Gatwick is an important adjunct to Heathrow, although considerably smaller—in 1977 only 5.9 million passengers used the facility. Some important supplemental airlines such as Laker land here. In addition, a massive improvement project is underway to expand airport services and increase traffic.

Location—Situated 30 miles south of London, Gatwick is served by excellent rail connections.

Transportation facilities—The best way to get to the airport is by rail. Those who drive or take a taxi do not gain in convenience or time.

Private automobiles—Private cars travel along A23 or M23 motorways. The long-term lot is connected to the terminal by a free shuttle service. The cost is £3.40 every three days, 85p per day from then on. Short-term lots are next to the terminal and cost 12p for the first hour, up to £2.20 a day. A moving sidewalk connects the lots to the terminal.

Taxi service—London taxis do not serve Gatwick. Suburban taxi service is available 24 hours a day from the desk in the international arrivals hall and costs 47 pence per mile.

Train service—The train from Victoria station is the best way to get to and from the airport and takes about 40 minutes. Departures are every 15 minutes during the day; once an hour at night. The cost for a second-class ticket is £1.50; for a first-class ticket, £3.

Hotel facilities—There are no hotel facilities on the airport grounds. Reservations can be made from the hotel bookings international desk in the arrivals hall. Call Crawley (0293) 302660.

Airport facilities and services—Gatwick is in the process of enormous expansion and renovation and will accommodate many more passengers and airlines in the near future. It is expected to help ease the load at Heathrow. The terminal now is basically housed in one three-story building—the international arrivals section is on two floors. The departures and domestic arrivals section is on the same floor as some of the international flight arrivals, and the third floor has a chapel, cocktail bar, coffee shops, restaurants and gift shops.

International flight arrivals—Ground Floor: This area contains immigration and arrivals areas. Concourse level: This area contains customs, baggage claim, a bank and access to departures and the railway station.

All flight departures and UK arrivals—This is the general service area, attached to the international arrivals section by escalators and elevator. It contains shops, a bank, restaurants, a bar and gift shops. The departure area contains check-in counters, passport control, duty-free shop, restaurant, bar, departure lounge and all boarding gates.

Airlines serving Gatwick. The following airlines fly in and out of Gatwick.

Aer Lingus	Dan Air
Aeroflot	IAS Cargo Services
Air Alsace	Index Adria
Air Malawi	Laker
Air Paris	Martinair
Aviaco	Monarch
Aviogenex Belgrade	NLM
Balair	Overseas National Airways
Braathens SAFE	Quebecair
British Airways	SATA
British Caledonian	Spantax
British Island	Sterling
British Midland	TAROM
Brittania Airways	TAP
Canadian Armed Forces	Tradewinds
Canadian Pacific	Trans International
Capitol International	Wardair Canada
Caribbean Airways	World

Note: If you are interested in investigating intra-European air fares while abroad, many of the airlines serving Gatwick can give you information.

Handicapped services are well thought out. The airport is designed with ramps and elevators in all areas, and special restrooms are located throughout the terminal. British Airways' *Carriage of Invalids by Air* is helpful. Another booklet, *Care in the Air,* published by the Airline Users Committee, may be obtained by writing to the committee at Space House, 43-59 Kingsway, London WC2, England.

Gatwick provides its own guide. You may obtain one by writing Airport Services, British Airports, 2 Buckingham Gate, London SW1E 6JL, England.

Special arrangements should be made through your travel agent, tour company or airline.

Medical facilities are available 24 hours a day in a clinic run by the Nursing Sisters. A doctor is always on call. There are *Medical Centre* signs throughout the building, which will guide you to the casualty unit situated on the catering level of the international arrivals hall.

Traveler's Aid does not maintain an office here.

PARIS AIRPORTS

Paris, like London, has several airports in the metropolitan area. Orly and DeGaulle are the two most important for the international traveler.

ORLY

The older of the two airports, Orly is a large and complex facility that is not easily negotiated. It is divided into two separate terminals known as Orly Sud (south) and Orly Ouest (west).

Location—Orly is situated nine miles south of Notre Dame Cathedral and 31 miles south of Charles de Gaulle Airport.

Transportation facilities—Car, taxi, bus and rail connections all serve Orly.

Private automobiles—Cars should allow at least 40 minutes to get from the center of Paris to Orly. To the airport—take autoroute du Sud A6 from Porte d'Orléans or RN7 from Porte d'Italie. From the airport—take the route marked Paris Ouest for Porte d'Orléans or Paris Est for Porte d'Italie.

Parking is available in three lots. Short-term lot P1 at Orly Sud has nearly 2,400 spaces and is located directly across from the terminal. It costs five francs per hour, 27 francs maximum a day. Lot PO at Orly Ouest has 3,600 spaces and costs the same. Lot P7 in the long-term lot has 1,300 spaces and is connected to both terminals by free shuttle bus. It costs a maximum of 13 francs a day. You may put your car in the lot 24 hours a day, but you cannot get it out between midnight and 7:00 A.M.

Bus service—To and from Paris, you can get an Air France bus from Les Invalides Terminal for 12 francs.

Allow 40 minutes. Service is from 7:00 A.M. to 10:40 P.M. every 15 minutes. The Air France bus is available between Orly and DeGaulle airports for 25 francs. Allow 75 minutes' traveling time. Service is every 30 minutes from 6:00 A.M. to 11:00 P.M.; thereafter as flights require it.

Train service—Orlyrail is a bus and train connection that runs from the airport to the Gare d'Austerlitz, Pont St Michel and Quai d'Orsay every 15 minutes from 5:30 A.M. until 9:00 P.M., then every 30 minutes after that. The trip takes about 40 minutes and costs about 11 francs.

Hotel facilities—Hotel facilities are available at the airport. A small hotel, Air Hotel, is in the Sud terminal. It has 56 rooms, and reservations can be made by calling 726-03-10.

The main hotel is the Hilton Orly, which has 388 rooms. There is a free shuttle to it from both terminals. Pick it up at Gate F, Orly Sud, or gate J Orly Ouest. Phone: 726-40-00.

The PLM Orly (687-23-37) is the second largest hotel with 200 rooms and is slightly less expensive than the Hilton Orly. Shuttle service is available from the same gates as for the Hilton.

Airport facilities and service—Orly is another enormous complex, as you can tell from the description of its terminals. These terminals have all the standard facilities: restaurants, shops, duty-free shops, flowers, books and candy stores, hairdressers, currency exchanges, medical units and nurseries.

Orly Sud is the international terminal. Its ground floor contains the check-in counters for most of the airlines plus baggage claim, customs, immigration, currency exchange, lost and found, a candy store, lost baggage area, car rental counter, ground transportation and lockers. Below it, in the first basement, is a bank, bar, post office, shops, lockers, dry cleaner, lottery, newsstand, photo shop, shoe repair, supermarket and hairdresser.

On the second floor, above the check-in counters, are duty-free shops, passport control, baths/showers, a chapel, nursery, restaurant and shops. On the third floor are a restaurant, bar, snack bar, and tearoom. On the fourth floor of Orly Sud are a movie theater and restaurant.

At Orly Ouest, on the ground floor, are the arrivals. This area contains customs, a lost and found, information desk, car rental, limousines, bank, currency exchange, baggage claim, showers, post office, hairdresser, ground transportation and hotel and theater reservations. On the first floor, departures, are immigration, shopping, shoe shine, insurance, nursery, medical center, chaplain, duty-free shop. On the second floor is a bar and restaurant.

Handicapped facilities are well-planned. In Orly Sud specially designed restrooms are on the first floor near the international zone. At Orly Ouest special restrooms are on the first floor in hall two and three. In both terminals departing passengers stop at gate N (Orly Sud) or gate W (Orly Ouest), where a special telephone there notifies airport staff who will meet you and help you get from the terminal to your gate. An airport service rep will provide arriving passengers with wheelchairs to get them to a car or taxi.

Medical facilities are available. At Orly Sud, service is provided from 7:00 A.M. to 11:00 P.M. and is located on the first floor near stairway S1. At Orly Ouest, for all medical emergencies in both terminals, call 687 12 34 24 hours a day, contact the airline or airport personnel or go to the departures level of the terminal. Vaccinations (687 23 34) are available for forgetful tourists.

Airlines serving Orly. The following airlines fly in and out of Orly:

Aer Lingus	Air Malta
Aeroflot	Air Rouergue
Aerolineas Argentinas	Alia
Aero Mexico	Alitalia
Air Algerie	Ariana Afghan
Air Ceylon	Austrian Airlines
Air France	Balkan
Air India	British Airways
Air Inter	British Midland
Air Madagascar	Cameroon Airways

Cyprus Airways	LOT
Czechoslovak Airlines	Lufthansa
East African Airways	Lybian Arab
Egyptair	Middle East
El Al	Olympic
Ethiopian Airlines	PIA
Europe Aeroservice	Qantas
Finnair	Royal Air Maroc
Gulf Air	Singapore Airlines
Iberia	South African Airways
Iran Air	Swissair
Iraqi Airways	Syrian Arab
JAL	TAP
JAT, Yugoslav	TAT
Korean	Tunis
Kuwait Airways	Varig
Lan-Chile	Viasa

CHARLES DE GAULLE AIRPORT

The newest of Paris's airports, DeGaulle, was opened in 1974. It is a vast and modern complex that makes use of moving sidewalks to make the distances less troublesome to the weary, disabled or rushed traveler.

Location—Situated 17 miles northeast of Notre Dame Cathedral, DeGaulle is easily reached by many forms of transportation.

Transportation facilities—Car, taxi, bus and train services can get you to the plane on time.

Private automobiles—Cars should travel along the autoroute du Nord from the Porte de la Chapelle or A3-B3, expressways from Porte de Bagnolet, or RN2 highway from Porte de la Villette. Allow 40 minutes traveling time. Add 20 minutes during rush hours.

Parking is plentiful. Short-term parking is right across from the terminal, where there are 3,800 parking spaces. The cost is five francs per hour with a 23 franc maximum a day. Long-term (Lot B) has 2,000 spaces and is connected to the terminal by free shuttle service. It costs 11 francs a day.

Taxi service—Taxis are available opposite gate 16 on the arrivals floor of the terminal building. The fare is about 50 francs to the Place de l'Opéra. You do *not* have to pay twice the meter although drivers sometimes ask for it.

Bus service—An Air France coach is available to and from the airport and runs every 15–20 minutes from 6:00 A.M. to 11:00 P.M. In Paris, the bus stops at Les Invalides or at Porte Maillot. At the airport, it stops outside the arrivals terminal. The cost is 10 francs. Allow 50 minutes' traveling time to Les Invalides, 30 minutes to Porte Maillot.

RATP bus service is provided by several lines. Number 350 bus from Gare du Nord takes 40 minutes and costs about 7.5 francs. Number 351 bus from Place de la Nation to DeGaulle takes 50–60 minutes and costs 7.5 francs. Service only during daytime hours.

Hotel facilities—There is the Jacques Borel Hotel on the airport grounds with 352 rooms (862 23 23). A shuttle ride of six minutes takes passengers to and from the terminal.

Airport facilities and services—DeGaulle is an airport that is beautiful to look at but pretty tough to figure out. It is based on the idea of satellite terminals, each connected to a main terminal by walkways, moving sidewalks, roads, elevators and special handicap access routes. The hub of the airport is called the *Boutiquaire* floor. It provides access to arrivals and departures, and it houses restaurants, shops of great variety and quality, a bank, post office and a telephone area. From that hub you can get to arrivals or departures.

The *arrival floor* contains customs, banks and all arrival gates.

Departure floors contain check-in desks and boarding gates, banks and insurance counters.

Satellite transfer floors (to Satellites 1–7): This structure is a central clearinghouse that contains customs and immigration, restaurants, banks, nursery and chapel.

Handicapped facilities are very modern. All special

needs should be arranged through your airline. Departing passengers should take a taxi or car to special telephone at Gate 12 parking area. Alert airport personnel of your arrival, and a Redcap will meet you with an electric wheelchair. Access to all areas is provided by elevators.

A post office, telephone booths and restrooms are designed for wheelchair access, and specially arranged showers for the handicapped are located on the transfer floor near satellites 3 and 4.

Medical center restrooms are located in the arrivals section and near satellites 3 and 4.

Medical facilities are located near the entrance hall on the Boutiquaire floor. For emergencies, contact any airport employee.

Airlines serving DeGaulle Airport. The following airlines fly in and out of DeGaulle Airport:

Air Afrique	British
Air Canada	British Caledonian
Air Ceylon	CAAC
Air France	JAL
Air Inter	Saudi Arabian
Air Mali	SAS
Air Zaïre	Sabena
Ariana Afghan	TWA
Avianca	UTA

LEONARDO DaVINCI AIRPORT

DaVinci airport, known also as Fumicino, is located 20 miles west of Rome, near the ancient town of Ostia Antiqua.

Transportation facilities—Bus, taxi and automobile are the easiest methods of travel between the airport and the city.

Private automobiles—Cars traveling from Rome should allow 75 minutes' traveling time. Parking is available in five lots. Rates are not available, but assume that the farther you are from the terminal the cheaper the parking. Taxis are available outside the terminal. Always ask the driver for a rate or estimate before getting into the cab.

Bus service—Intermezzo bus lines provide service from the main Rome hotels and run every 45 minutes from 7:15 A.M. to midnight, daily. Allow at least one hour traveling time.

Acotral buses leave the main terminal station every 15 minutes from 7:00 A.M. to 7:00 P.M., and every 30 minutes from 7:00 P.M. to 7:00 A.M. The cost is 1000 lire.

Airport facilities and services—Remodeled and expanded over the years, DaVinci, or Fumicino, as it used to be called, is divided into two terminals, international and domestic.

In the international terminal, the first floor arrivals area has customs, passport control, baggage claim area, bank, first aid, public health control, hotel reservations and car rental counters. The second floor departure area has a duty-free shop, check-in counters, ticket counters, snack bars and shops, an information counter, passport control area and boarding gates.

In the domestic terminal, the first floor has both arrivals and departures facilities: the second floor has duty-free shops and passport control.

Handicapped facilities should be arranged through the individual airlines. There is access to all parts of the airport, and the staff at the first-aid station will assist any traveler with personal needs.

Medical facilities are in the first-aid station on the ground floor, near the entrance to domestic gates 8–14. Serious medical problems should be reported to any airport employee.

Airlines serving DaVinci. The following airlines fly into and out of DaVinci:

Aer Lingus	Air Algerie
Aero Trasporti Italiani	Air France
Aeroflot Soviet	Air Gabon
Aerolineas Argentinas	Air India
Air Afrique	Air Madagascar

Air Malta
Air Mauritius
Air Zaire
Alia-Royal Jordanian
Alisarda
Alitalia
Ariana Afghan
Austrian
Avianca
Avic Ligure S.P.A.
British
Bulgarian—Balkan
Cameroon
CP
Czechoslovak
Deta
Egyptair
El Al Israel
Ethiopian
Finnair
Garuda Indonesian
Ghana
Iberia
Iran National
Iraqi
Itavia
Japan
Kenya
KLM-Royal Dutch
Kuwait
Libyan Arab

Lot Polish
Lufthansa
Luxair-Luxembourg
Malev-Hungarian
Middle East
Nigeria
Olympic
Pakistan International
Pan American World
Philippine
Qantas
Royal Air Maroc
Sabena Belgian
SAS-Scandinavian
Saudi Arabian
Singapore
Somali
South African
Sudan
Swissair
Syrian Arab
Tarom-Romanian
Thai International
Trans World
Tunis
Turk Hava Yollari
Varig
Viasa
Yemen
Yugoslav (JAT)
Zambia

APPENDIX A
TRAVELER'S AIDS

TIME DIFFERENCES—WORLD CITIES

At 12:00 P.M. Eastern Standard Time, the time in the following cities is as follows:

*Indicates morning of the following day.

Alexandria	7:00 P.M.
Amsterdam	6:00 P.M.
Athens	7:00 P.M.
Atlanta	12:00 P.M.
Auckland	5:00 A.M.*
Baghdad	8:00 P.M.
Bangkok	12:00 A.M.
Belfast	5:00 P.M.
Berlin	6:00 P.M.
Bogota	12:00 P.M.
Boise	10:00 A.M.
Bombay	10:30 P.M.
Bremen	6:00 P.M.
Brussels	6:00 P.M.
Bucharest	7:00 P.M.
Budapest	6:00 P.M.
Buenos Aires	2:00 P.M.
Calcutta	10:30 P.M.
Cape Town	7:00 P.M.

Caracas	1:00 P.M.
Chicago	11:00 A.M.
Copenhagen	6:00 P.M.
Dacca	11:00 P.M.
Delhi	10:30 P.M.
Denver	10:00 A.M.
Djakarta	12:00 A.M.
Dublin	5:00 P.M.
Gdansk	6:00 P.M.
Geneva	6:00 P.M.
Havana	12:00 P.M.
Helsinki	7:00 P.M.
Hong Kong	1:00 A.M.*
Honolulu	7:00 A.M.
Istanbul	7:00 P.M.
Jerusalem	7:00 P.M.
Johannesburg	7:00 P.M.
Kansas City	11:00 A.M.
Karachi	10:00 P.M.
Le Havre	6:00 P.M.
Leningrad	8:00 P.M.
Lima	12:00 P.M.
Lisbon	6:00 P.M.
Liverpool	5:00 P.M.
London	5:00 P.M.
Los Angeles	9:00 A.M.
Madrid	6:00 P.M.
Manila	1:00 A.M.*
Melbourne	3:00 A.M.*
Montevideo	2:00 P.M.
Montreal	12:00 P.M.
Moscow	8:00 P.M.
Nagasaki	2:00 A.M.*
New York	12:00 P.M.
Oslo	6:00 P.M.
Paris	6:00 P.M.
Peking	1:00 A.M.*
Prague	6:00 P.M.

Rangoon	11:30 P.M.
Rio De Janeiro	2:00 P.M.
Rome	6:00 P.M.
Saigon	1:00 A.M.*
Salt Lake City	10:00 A.M.
Santiago	1:00 P.M.
Seoul	2:00 A.M.*
Shanghai	1:00 A.M.*
Singapore	12:30 A.M.*
Stockholm	6:00 P.M.
Sydney	3:00 A.M.*
Tashkent	11:00 P.M.
Teheran	8:30 P.M.
Tel Aviv	7:00 P.M.
Tokyo	2:00 A.M.*
Valparaiso	1:00 P.M.
Vancouver	9:00 A.M.
Vladivostok	3:00 A.M.*
Vienna	6:00 P.M.
Warsaw	6:00 P.M.
Wellington	5:00 A.M.*
Wichita	11:00 A.M.
Yokohama	2:00 A.M.*
Zurich	6:00 P.M.

U.S. EMBASSIES & CONSULATES

Country	Address	Tel. Nos.
Austria	9 Boltzmanngasse 16, Vienna	346611
Belgium	27 Boulevard du Regent, Brussels	133830
Bulgaria	1 Alexander Stamboliski Boulevard, Sofia	884801
Czechoslovakia	Trziste 15, 12548 Prague	536641
Denmark	Dag Hammarskjolds Alle 24, Copenhagen	123144
Finland	Itainen Kaivopuisto 21, Helsinki	11931
France	2 Avenue Gabriel 75382, Paris	2657460
Germany	Mehlemer Avenue, Bad Godesberg, Bonn	1955
Great Britain	24 Grosvenor Square, W.I., London	4999000
Greece	91 Vasilissis Sophias Boulevard, Athens	712951
Hungary	V. Szabadsag Ter. 12, Budapest	329375
Ireland	42 Elgin Road, Ballsbridge, Dublin	64061
Israel	71 Hayarkon Street, Tel Aviv	56171
Italy	Via Veneto 119, Rome	4674
Lebanon	Corniche at Rue Ain Mreisseh Beirut	240800
Luxembourg	22 Boulevard Emmanuel Servais, Luxembourg	40123
Morocco	2 Avenue de Marrakech, Rabat	30361
Netherlands	Museumplein 19, Amsterdam	790321
Norway	Drammensveien 18, Oslo	566880
Poland	Aleje Ujazdowskie 29/31, Warsaw	283041

Portugal	Avenue Duque de Loule 39, Lisbon	555141
Romania	Str. Tudor Argezhi 9, Bucharest	124040
Russia	Ulitsa Chaykovskogo 19/21/23, Moscow	2520011
South Africa ..	521 South African Mutual Building, Johannesburg	8343051
Spain	Serrano 75, Madrid	2763400
Sweden	Strandvagen 101, Stockholm	630520
Switzerland ...	93 Jubilaumsstrasse, Bern	430011
Turkey	110 Ataturk Boulevard, Ankara	186200
Yugoslavia	Kneza Milosa 50, Belgrade	645655

WEIGHTS & MEASURES

WEIGHTS Metric Equivalent

U.S.A.

ounce	= 28.35 grams	1 gram	= .04 ounce
pound	= .45 kilogram	1 kilogram	= 2.20 pounds
ton	= .91 metric ton	1 metric ton	= 1.10 tons

LIQUID MEASURE Metric Equivalent

U.S.A.

pint	= .47 liter	1 liter = 2.11 pints
quart	= .95 liter	1 liter = 1.06 quarts
gallon	= 3.79 liters	1 liter = .26 gallons

LENGTH Metric Equivalent

U.S.A.

inch	= 2.54 centimeters
foot	= .30 meter
yard	= .91 meter
mile	= 1.61 kilometers
.39 inch	= 1 centimeter
3.28 feet	= 1 meter
1.09 yards	= 1 meter
.62 mile	= 1 kilometer

To convert from kilometers to miles, divide the number of kilometers by 8 and multiply the result by 5.

TEMPERATURE

To Compute Fahrenheit: Multiply Centigrade by 1.8 and add 32.

To Compute Centigrade: Subtract 32 from Fahrenheit and divide by 1.8.

Centi-grade		Fahren-heit
100°	=	212°
	Boiling point	
90°	=	194°
80°	=	176°
70°	=	158°
60°	=	140°
50°	=	122°
40°	=	104°
37°	=	98°
	Normal body temp	
30°	=	86°
20°	=	68°
10°	=	50°
5°	=	41°
0°	=	32°
	Freezing point	

CLOTHING SIZES

DRESSES, SUITS AND COATS

American:	8	10	12	14	16	18
British:	30	32	34	36	38	40
Continental:	36	38	40	42	44	46

BLOUSES AND SWEATERS

American:	32	34	36	38	40	42	44
British:	34	36	38	40	42	44	46
Continental:	40	42	44	46	48	50	52

DRESSES AND COATS (Children's and Junior Misses)

American:	2	4	6	8	10	13	15
British & Continental:	1	2	5	7	9	10	12

STOCKINGS

American and British:	8	8½	9	9½	10	10½	11
Continental:	35	36	37	38	39	40	41

SHOES

American:	5	5½	6	6½	7	7½	8	8½	9
British:	3½	4	4½	5	5½	6	6½	7	7½
Continental:	35	35	36	37	38	38	38½	39	40

GLOVE sizes are the same as in the U.S.A.

SUITS, SWEATERS AND OVERCOATS

American and British:	34	36	38	40	42	44	46	48
Continental:	44	46	48	50	52	54	56	58

SHIRTS

American and British:	14	14½	15	15½	16	16½	17	17½
Continental:	36	37	38	39	40	41	42	43

SOCKS

American and British:	9½	10	10½	11	11½	12	12½
Continental:	39	40	41	42	43	44	45

SHOES

American:	7	7½	8	8½	9	9½	10	10½	11	11½
British:	6½	7	7½	8	8½	9	9½	10	10½	11
Continental:	39	40	41	42	43	43	44	44	45	45

MEN'S HATS

American:	6⅝	6¾	6⅞	7	7⅛	7¼	7⅜	7½	7⅝
British:	6½	6⅝	6¾	6⅞	7	7⅛	7¼	7⅜	7½
Continental:	53	54	55	56	57	58	59	60	61

GLOVE sizes are the same as in the U.S.A.

(All size equivalents are approximate)

APPENDIX B
AIRLINES' ADDRESSES
AND
TELEPHONE NUMBERS

Here is a list of many of the world's scheduled airline companies and their codes, headquarter addresses and telephone numbers. This list is useful for tracking down information about travel within foreign countries, in exotic locales, and on unusual airlines. Additionally, you can find out where to write if you need to send a complaint to the executives of a company.

AER LINGUS TEORANTA (Irish International) (EI)
Dublin Airport
P.O.B. 180
Dublin, Ireland
Tel. 370011

AEROCONDOR—Aerovias Condor de Colombia Ltd. (OD)
Carrera 45B
(P.O. Box 2299)
Barranquilla, Colombia
Tel. 27700

AEROFLOT—Soviet Airlines (SU)
Leningradsky Prospekt, 37
Moscow, U.S.S.R.
Tel. 83-58-35

AEROLINEAS ARGENTINAS (AR)
Paseo Colon 185
Buenos Aires, Argentina
Tel. 30-2071

AEROMEXICO (AM)
Boulevard Aeropuerto Central 161
Mexico City, Mexico
Tel. 903—571-3000

AEROPERU (PL)
Cailloma 818 (P12)
Lima, Peru
Tel. 27-6200

AEROVIAS NACIONALES DE HONDURAS (See SAHSA)

AIR AFRIQUE (RK)
Box 21-017
Abidjan, Ivory Coast, West Africa
Tel. 22-60-63

AIR ALGERIE (See CGTA)

AIR ALSACE (SY)
68000 Aerodrome de Colmar-Houssen
Colmar, France
Tel. (89) 41.43.95

AIR BVI, LTD. (BL)
Box 85, Roadtown
Tortola, British Virgin Islands
Tel. 5-2346

AIR CANADA (AC)
Place Ville Marie
Montreal 113.
Quebec, Canada
Tel. 514/874-4560

AIR CEYLON LIMITED (AE)
P.O. Box 692
Sir D.B. Jayatileke
Mawatha, Colombo 1, Sri Lanka
Tel. 27731-34

AIR FRANCE (AF)
1 Square Max Hymans

Paris 75015, France
Tel. 273-41-41
AIR INDIA (AI)
218 Backbay Reclamation
Nariman Point
Bombay 400 001, India
Tel. 292728
AIR INTER—Lignes Aeriennes Interieures (IT)
1 Avenue Du Marechal Devaux
F 91550 Paray Vieille Poste
France
Tel. 687-12-12
AIR JAMAICA LIMITED (JM)
72-76 Harbour Street
Kingston, Jamaica, W.I.
Tel. 932-3460
AIR LIBERIA, INC. (NL)
P.O. Box 2076
Monrovia, Liberia
Tel. 22144
AIR MALAWI (QM)
Robins Road, (P.O.B. 84)
Blantyre, Malawi
Tel. Blantyre 2001
AIR MALI (MY)
P.O. Box 27
Bamako
Republic of Mali
Tel. 27-41/2, 35-36, 33-36
AIR MALTA COMPANY, LTD.—Air Malta (KM)
Development House
St. Anne Street
Floriana, Malta
Tel. 21421
AIR MAURITIUS (MK)
1 Sir William Street
Port Louis, Mauritius
Tel. 1286
AIR MICRONESIA (See Continental Airlines)

AIR MIDWEST (ZV)
Hangar No. 17
Municipal Airport
Wichita, Kansas 67209
Tel. 316-942-1223
AIR NAURU (ON)
Republic of Nauru
Nauru Island
Central Pacific
AIR NEW ENGLAND (NE)
Logan International Airport
East Boston, Massachusetts 02128
Tel. 617-569-5650
AIR NEW ZEALAND—INTERNATIONAL (TE)
Private Bag
Auckland 1
New Zealand
Tel. 78-919
DOMESTIC (NZ)
New Zealand Division
70 The Terrace (P.O. Box 96)
Wellington, C.1. New Zealand
Tel. 725-699
AIR PACIFIC (FJ)
Box 112
Suva, Fiji Islands
Tel. 25-661
AIR PANAMA INTERNACIONAL (OP)
Ave. Justo Arosemena y Calle 34
Panama City, Panama Rep.
Tel. 25-8389, 25-3961
AIR PARIS (IO)
c/o Touraine Air Transport
Aeroport de Tours
B.P. 208
37001 Tours, France
Tel. (47) 54.21.45
AIR RHODESIA (RH)
P.O. Box AP1

Salisbury Airport
Salisbury, Rhodesia
Tel. 52601
AIR ZAIRE (QC)
4 Avenue du Port
(P.O. Box 8552)
Kinshasa, Zaire
Tel. 76031 & 76131
ALASKA AIRLINES, INC. (AS)
Seattle-Tacoma International Airport
Seattle, Washington 98158
Tel. 206—433-3200
ALIA—The Royal Jordanian Airlines (RJ)
El Fayez Bldg.
Prince Hassan St. (P.O.B. 302)
Amman, Jordan
Tel. 22314, 22315, 22316
ALITALIA—Linee Aeree Italiane (AZ)
Palazzo Alitalia
Piazza Guido Pastore
00144 Rome, Italy
Tel. 54441
ALLEGHENY AIRLINES, INC (AL)
Washington Nat'l Airport
Washington, D.C. 20001
Tel. 202—892-7000
ALL NIPPON AIRWAYS COMPANY, LTD. (NH)
Kasumigaseki Bldg., 3-2-5
Kasumigaseki
Chiyoda-Ku
Tokyo, Japan
Tel. 580-4711
ALM—Antillean Airlines (LM)
Dr. Albert Plesman Airport
Curacao, Netherlands, Antilles
Tel. 81322
ALOHA AIRLINES, INC. (TS)
222 Alexander Young Building
Honolulu, Hawaii 96813

Tel. 842-4101

AMERICAN AIRLINES, INC. (AA)
633 Third Avenue
New York, New York 10017
Tel. 212—557-1234

ANHSA (Aerovias Nacionales de Honduras) (See SAHSA)

ANSETT AIRLINES OF AUSTRALIA (AN)
489 Swanston St.
Melbourne C.I.
Victoria, Australia
Tel. 345-1211

ARIANA AFGHAN AIRLINES (FG)
Jadde Maiwand
(P.O. Box 76)
Kabul, Afghanistan
Tel. 25541, 26541

ARROW AVIATION, LTD. (DG)
R.R.3
Kelowna Airport
Kelowna, B.C. Canada V2S 4N9
Tel. 604-765-5567

ASPEN AIRWAYS, INC. (AP)
Hangar No. 5
Stapleton International Airport
Denver, Colorado 80207
Tel. 303-398-3745

AUSTRIAN AIRLINES (OS)
Salesianergasse 1
Vienna 3, Austria
Tel. 73-65-65

AVIACO—Aviacion Y Comercio, S.A. (AO)
Maudes, 51
Madrid 3
Spain
Tel. 254 36 00 Centralita

AVIANCA—Aerovias Nacionales de Colombia, S.A. (AV)
Centro Administrativo

Avenida El Dorado #93-30
Bogota, Colombia, S.A.
Tel. 82-01-00
AVIATECA—Empresa Guatemalteca de Aviacion (GU)
Ave. Hincapie Aeropuerto "La Aurora"
Guatemala City
Guatemala
Tel. 63-2-27, 63-2-28, 63-5-76, 61-9-74
BAHAMASAIR (UP)
P.O. Box 592736
Miami Int'l Airport
Miami, Florida 33159
Tel. 305—379-2843
BEA (See British Airways)
BOAC (See British Airways)
BRAATHENS S.A.F.E. AIRTRANSPORT (BU)
Ruselokkveien 26
Oslo 2, Norway
Tel. 332190
BRANIFF INTERNATIONAL AIRWAYS (BN)
Exchange Park
(P.O. Box 35001)
Dallas, Texas 75235
Tel. 214—358-6011
BRITISH AIRWAYS (BA, BE)
P.O. Box 10
Heathrow Airport
Hounslow TW6 2JA, England
Tel. 01-759-5511
BRITISH CALEDONIAN AIRWAYS (BR)
Gatwick Airport-London
Horley, Surrey, RH6 OLT, England
Tel. 01-283-8755
BRITISH ISLAND AIRWAYS, LTD. (UK)
Berkeley House
5153 High Street
Redhill, Surrey RH1 1RX
England
Tel. Redhill 65941

BRITISH MIDLAND AIRWAYS (BD)
East Midlands Airport
Castle Donington
Derby, England
Tel. 471/8

BRITISH WEST INDIAN AIRWAYS, LTD. (BW)
Kent House
Long Circular Road
Maraval
Port of Spain, Trinidad, W.I.
Tel. 21241

CAMEROON AIRLINES (UY)
3 Avenue de Gaulle
B.P. 4092
Douala, Cameroon
Tel. 42-25-25

CARIBBEAN AIRWAYS (IQ)
Seawell International Airport
Christchurch
Barbados, W.I.
Tel. 87101

CATHAY PACIFIC AIRWAYS, LTD. (CX)
Union House
9 Connaught Road Central
Hong Kong, Hong Kong
Tel. H-250011

CAYMAN AIRWAYS, LTD. (KX)
P.O. Box 11
Grand Cayman, B.W.I.
Tel. 9-2311

CGTA—Companie Generale de Transports Aeriens-Air Algeria (AH)
1 Place Maurice Audin
Immeuble El-Djezair
Algiers, Algeria
Tel. 639234/36

CHINA AIR LINES LTD. (CI)
26, Sec. III, Nanking East Rd.
Taipei, Taiwan

Tel. 571-1111, 571-9111
COMAIR—Commercial Airways (Pty.) Ltd. (MN)
P.O. Box 2245
Johannesburg, 2000
Transvaal, South Africa
Tel. 21-5975
CONTINENTAL AIRLINES INC. (CO)
International Airport
Los Angeles, Calif. 90009
Tel. 213—646-2810
CP AIR (CP)
One Grant McConachie Way
Vancouver International Airport
Vancouver B.C., Canada V7B 1V1
Tel. 604-273-1484
CRUZEIRO DO SUL S.A. SERVICOS AEREOS, (SC)
128 Avenida Rio Branco
(P.O.B. 190)
Rio de Janeiro, Brazil
Tel. 224-0522
CSA—Ceskoslovenske Aerolinie (OK)
Revolucni 1
16015 Prague, Czechoslovakia
Tel. 2146
**CUBANA—Empresa Consolidada Cubana de Aviacion
(CU)**
Calle 23 No. 64, La Rampa
Vedado
Havana 4, Cuba
Tel. 7-4911
CYPRUS AIRWAYS, LTD. (CY)
21 Athanasiou Dhiakou Str.
Nicosia, Cyprus
Tel. 43054
CZECHOSLOVAK AIRLINES (See CSA)
DANAIR (DX)
c/o Scandinavian Airlines System
DAN-AIR SERVICES, LTD. (DA)
Bilbao House

36-38 New Broad Street
London EC2M 1NH, England
Tel. 01-283-4288
DELTA AIR LINES, INC. (DL)
Hartsfield Atlanta Airport
Atlanta, Georgia 30320
Tel. 404-346-6011
DETA—Linhas Aereas de Mozambique (TM)
Av. do General Machado N°2-2°
(P.O. Box 2060)
Maputo, Mozambique
Tel. 27045/732141
DOMINICANA DE AVIACION (DO)
El Conde 83
Apartado 322
Santo Domingo, Dominican Rep.
Tel. 2-6094, 2-6098
DOUGLAS AIRWAYS PTY., LTD. (DZ)
P.O. Box 1179
Boroko, Moresby
Papua New Guinea
Tel. 53499
EASTERN AIR LINES, INC. (EA)
10 Rockefeller Plaza
New York, N.Y. 10020
Tel. 212—956-4000
EASTERN PROVINCIAL AIRWAYS, LTD. (PV)
P.O. Box 5001
Gander, Newfoundland, Canada A1V 1W9
Tel. 709—256-3941
EAST-WEST AIRLINES, LTD. (EW)
323 Castlereagh
Sydney, Australia
Tel. Sydney 20940
ECUADORIAN AIRLINES (See Empresa Ecuatoriana de Aviacion)
ECUATORIANA (See Empresa Ecuatoriana de Aviacion)

EGYPTAIR (MS)
Almaza Airport
Heliopolis
Cairo, Egypt
Tel. 64255/9
EL AL ISRAEL AIRLINES LTD. (LY)
Lod Airport
Tel-Aviv, Israel
Tel. 971333
EMPRESA ECUATORIANA DE AVIACION (EU)
Jorge Washington
718 Y Amazonas
P.O. Box 505
Quito, Ecuador
Tel. 541-222
ETHIOPIAN AIR LINES (ET)
P.O. Box 1755
Addis Ababa, Ethiopia
Tel. 52222
FAUCETT—Compania de Aviacion "Faucett", S.A. (CF)
Jiron Union No. 926
Lima, Peru
Tel. 51-3484
FIJI AIR (PC)
Fiji Trading Co. Bldg.
P.O. Box 1259
Victoria Parade
Suva, Fiji
Tel. Suva 22 666-7
FINNAIR (AY)
Mannerheimintie 102, 00250
Helsinki 25, Finland
Tel. 90/410411
FRONTIER AIRLINES INC. (FL)
8250 Smith Road
Denver, Colorado 80207
Tel. 303—398-5151

GARUDA INDONESIAN AIRWAYS (GA)
15 Djalan Nusantara
Jakarta, Indonesia
Tel. 40041/5
GHANA AIRWAYS (GH)
Ghana House
P.O. Box 1636
Accra, Ghana
Tel. 64851
GIBRALTAR AIRWAYS (GT)
Cloister Building
Market Lane
Gibraltar
Tel. 2151
GREAT LAKES AIRLINES, LTD. (GX)
Suite 1100
380 Wellington Street
London, Ontario, Canada N6A 585
Tel. 519-679-8540
GULF AIR (In Association with British Airways) (GF)
P.O. Box 138
Manama, Bahrain, Arabian Gulf
Tel. 51221
GUYANA AIRWAYS CORPORATION (GY)
P.O. Box 102
Georgetown, Guyana
Tel. 2455
HAWAIIAN AIRLINES (HA)
Honolulu Int'l Airport
P.O. Box 30008
Honolulu, Hawaii 96820
Tel. 808-525-5511
HUGHES AIRWEST (RW)
San Francisco International Airport
San Francisco, California 94128
Tel. 415—573-4000
IBERIA—Lineas Aereas de Espana, S.A. (IB)

Calle Velazquez 130
Madrid 6, Spain
Tel. 2619100-2619500
ICELANDAIR (Flugfelag Islands H.F.) (FI)
1 Hagatorg, (P.O. Box 1426)
Reykjavik, Iceland
Tel. 1-6600
**ICELANDIC AIRLINES (See Loftieidir Icelandic Air-
lines)**
INDIAN AIRLINES CORPORATION (IC)
Airlines House
113 Gurdwara Rakabganj Road
New Delhi, India
Tel. 388951
IRAN NATIONAL AIRLINES CORP. (IR)
Mehrabad Airport
Tehran, Iran
Tel. 9111
IRAQI AIRWAYS (IA)
Iraqi Airway Building
Baghdad International Airport
Baghdad, Iraq
Tel. 519999
JAPAN AIR LINES COMPANY, LTD. (JL)
Tokyo Bldg.
7-3 Marunouchi
2 Chome Chiyoda-Ku
Tokyo 100, Japan
Tel. (03) 284-2081
JAT (See Yugoslav Airlines)
KAR-AIR (KR)
c/o Finnair
Mannerheimtie 102
00250 Helsinki 25, Finland
KENYA AIRWAYS (KQ)
P.O. Box 19002
Nairobi, Kenya

Tel. 822171
**K.L.M.—Royal Dutch Airlines
(Koninklijke Luchtvaart Maatschappij) (KL)**
Schiphol International Airport
P.O. Box 7700
Netherlands
Tel. Amsterdam 020-499123
KODIAK WESTERN ALASKA AIRLINES (KO)
P.O. Box 2457
Kodiak, Alaska 99615
Tel. 907-486-3271
KOREAN AIR LINES (KE)
KAL BLDG.
118, 2-KA
Namdaemun-RO
Chung-Ku
P.O. Box 864 Central
Seoul, Korea
Tel. 28-2221
KUWAIT AIRWAYS (KU)
P.O. Box 394
Fahad As-Salem Str.
Kuwait, Arabian Gulf
Tel. 711166
LAB (See Lloyd Aereo Boliviano)
LACSA—Lineas Aereas Costarricenses, S.A. (LR)
P.O. Box 1531
San Jose, Costa Rica
Tel. 32-35-55
LADECO—Linea Aerea del Cobre (UC)
Aeroport Los Cerrillos
"HUERFANOS 1369"
P.O. Box 13740
Santiago, Chile
Tel. 571559
LAKER AIRWAYS LTD. (GK)
Gatwick Airport London
Horley, Surrey

England
Tel. (01) 668-9363
LAN CHILE—Linea Aerea Nacional de Chile (LA)
Casilla (P.O. Box) 147-D
Santiago, Chile
Tel. 572233
LANICA—Lineas Aereas de Nicaragua, S.A. (NI)
Apartado 753, Managua, Nicaragua
Tel. 22476
LANSA AIRLINES OF HONDURAS (UL)
Apartado Postal No. 35
La Ceiba, Honduras
Tel. 211
LIAT (1974) LTD. (LI)
Coolidge Airport
Antigua, West Indies
Tel. 20700
LIBERIAN NATIONAL AIR LINES INC. (See Air Liberia)
LIBYAN ARAB AIRLINES (LN)
P.O. Box 2555
Tripoli, Arab Republic of Libya
Tel. Tripoli 36021-29
LINEA AEROPOSTAL VENEZOLANA (LV)
Centro Capriles Plaza Venezuela
Caracas, Venezuela
Tel. 781-1111
LLOYD AEREO BOLIVIANO (LB)
Casilla 132
Cochabamba, Bolivia
Tel. 5911,5912,5913
LOFTLEIDIR ICELANDIC AIRLINES, INC. (LL)
Reykjavik Airport
Reykjavik, Iceland
Tel. 20-200
LOT—Polish Airlines (LO)
Grojecka 17
Warsaw, Poland

Tel. 223021
LUFTHANSA—German Airlines (LH)
Von-Gablenz-Str. 2-6
5 Cologne 21, Germany
Tel. (0221) 82 61
LUXAIR—S.A. Luxembourgeoise de Navigation Aerienne (LG)
Luxembourg Airport
Luxembourg
Tel. 47981
MALAYSIAN AIRLINE SYSTEM (MH)
P.O. Box 513
4 Jalan Sulaiman
Kuala Lumpur
Malaysia
Tel. 208844
MALEV—Hungarian Airlines (MA)
5 Vorosmarty-ter.
1051 Budapest, Hungary
Tel. 188-860
MEXICANA DE AVIACION, S.A. (MX)
Balderas 36
12th Floor
Mexico City, D.F., Mexico
Tel. 903-5-18-04-27
MIDDLE EAST AIRLINES/AIRLIBAN (ME)
Int'l Airport (P.O. Box 206)
Beirut, Lebanon
Tel. 272220, 292220, 292400
MT. COOK AIRLINES (NM)
47 Riccarton Road
Private Bag
Christchurch, New Zealand
MUNZ NORTHERN AIRLINES INC. (XY)
P.O. Box 790
Nome, Alaska 99763
Tel. 907-443-2215
NATIONAL AIRLINES, INC. (NA)
Airport Mail Facility (P.O. Box 2055)

Miami, Florida 33159
Tel. 305—874-4111
NEW YORK AIRWAYS, INC. (NY)
LaGuardia Airport Station
P.O. Box 426
Flushing, New York 11371
Tel. 212—DE 5-6600
NEW ZEALAND NATIONAL AIRWAYS CORP.
(See Air New Zealand—Domestic)
NIGERIA AIRWAYS LTD. (WT)
Airways House
Airport (P.O. Box 136)
Lagos, Nigeria
Tel. 31031
NLM DUTCH AIRLINES (HN)
Schiphol Airport
Amsterdam, Netherlands
NORCANAIR (See North Canada Air Ltd.)
NORDAIR, LTD. (ND)
P.O. Box 4000
Montreal Int'l Airport
Dorval, Quebec
Canada H4Y 1B8
Tel. 514—747-5592
NORTH CANADA AIR LTD. (NORCANAIR) (NK)
P.O. Box 850
Prince Albert, Sask.
Canada
Tel. 306-764-4271
NORTH CENTRAL AIRLINES, LTD. (NC)
7500 Northliner Drive
Minneapolis, Minnesota 55450
Tel. 612—726-7411
NORTHWEST ORIENT AIRLINES INC. (NW)
Minneapolis-St. Paul International Airport
St. Paul, Minnesota 55111
Tel. 612—726-2111
OLYMPIC AIRWAYS (OA)
96 Syngrou Ave.

Athens 404, Greece
Tel. 92921
OZARK AIR LINES, INC. (OZ)
Lambert Field
St. Louis, Missouri 63415
Tel. 314—895-6600
PACIFIC WESTERN AIRLINES, LTD. (PW)
Vancouver International Airport
Vancouver, B.C., Canada
Tel. 604—CR 3-6262
PAKISTAN INTERNATIONAL AIRLINES (PK)
PIA Building
Karachi Airport
Karachi, Pakistan
Tel. 412011
PAN AMERICAN WORLD AIRWAYS (PA)
PAN AM Building
200 Park Ave.
New York, N.Y. 10017
Tel. 212—973-7700
PEM AIR LIMITED (PD)
Pembroke Aerea Municipal Airport
R.R.6, Pembroke, Ontario
Canada K8A 6W7
Tel. 613-687-5579
PHILIPPINE AIR LINES (PR)
6780 Ayala Avenue
PAL Bldg.
Makati, Rizal, Philippines
Tel. 88-10-61
PIEDMONT AVIATION, INC. (PI)
Smith Reynolds Airport
Winston-Salem
North Carolina 27102
Tel. 919—767-5100
POLYNESIAN AIRLINES LTD. (PH)
Aircenter Beach Road
(P.O. Box 599)

Apia, Western Samoa
Tel. 740-743
QANTAS AIRWAYS, LTD. (QF)
Qantas House
70 Hunter St.
(P.O. Box 489)
Sydney, N.S.W., Australia
Tel. 230 0699
QUEBECAIR INC. (QB)
P.O. Box 490
Montreal International Airport
Dorval, Quebec, H4Y 1B5, Canada
Tel. 514—631-9802
REEVE ALEUTIAN AIRWAYS, INC. (RV)
P.O. Box 559
Anchorage, Alaska 99510
Tel. 272-9426
ROYAL AIR MAROC (AT)
Aeroport Anfa
Casablanca, Morocco
Tel. 523-84, 524-35
ROYAL DUTCH AIRLINES (See KLM)
ROYAL JORDANIAN AIRLINES (See Alia)
SABENA BELGIAN WORLD AIRLINES (SN)
(Societe Anonyme Belge d'Exploitation de la Navigation
Aerienne)
35 Rue Cardinal Mercier
1000, Brussels, Belgium
Tel. 511-9060
SAHSA—Servicio Aereo de Honduras, S.A. (SH)
P.O. Box 129
Tegucigalpa, D.C.
Honduras, C.A.
Tel. 22-0490, 22-4656, 22-8634
SAS (See Scandinavian Airlines System)
**SATA—Sociedade Acoriana de Transportes Aereos,
Lda. (SP)**
Av Infante D. Henrique

Ponta Delgada S. Miguel
Azores (Portugal)
Tel. 22311/2/3/4/5
SAUDI ARABIAN AIRLINES (SV)
Saudia Building
P.O. Box 620
Jeddah, Saudi Arabia
Tel. 25222 (ten lines)
SCANDINAVIAN AIRLINES SYSTEM (SK)
Ulvsundavagen 193
S-161 87 Stockholm-Bromma, Sweden
Tel. 780 10 00
SOLOMON ISLANDS AIRWAYS LTD. (IE)
P.O. Box 23
Honiara
Solomon Islands, Pacific Ocean
SOUTH AFRICAN AIRWAYS (SA)
South African Airways Centre
Johannesburg, Rep. of South Africa
Tel. 23-69-51
SOUTHERN AIRWAYS LTD. (SO)
Atlanta Airport
Atlanta, Georgia 30320
Tel. 404—766-5321
SUDAN AIRWAYS (SD)
Gamma Avenue
(P.O.B. 253)
Khartoum, Sudan
Tel. 74171
SUIDWES LUGDIENS (EDMS) BEPERK (SW)
Airport (P.O. Box 731)
Windhoek, South West Africa
Tel. 4451
SWISSAIR—Swiss Air Transport Co., Ltd. (SR)
P.O. Box 8058
Zurich, Switzerland
Tel. 812 12 12
SYRIAN ARAB AIRLINES (RB)
P.O. Box 417

Damascus, Syrian Arab Republic
Tel. 223434/5/6
TAA (See Trans-Australia Airlines)
TAAG-ANGOLA AIRLINES (DT)
Roa. Luis de Camoes, 123
Luanda, Angola
Tel. 72981/2/3/4
TACA INTERNATIONAL AIRLINES, S.A. (TA)
Edificio Caribe 20
San Salvador, El Salvador
Tel. 23-2244
TALAIR PTY. LTD. (GV)
P.O. Box 108
Goroka
Papua, New Guinea
Tel. 23/30/192
TAN AIRLINES—Transportes Aereos Nacionales, S.A. (TX)
Edificio Salame
Tegucigalpa, Honduras
Tel. 286 74/5
TAP—Transportes Aereos Portugueses, (TP)
Building 27
Lisbon Airport
P.O. Box 5194
Lisbon 5, Portugal
Tel. 719121
TAROM—Romanian Air Transport (RO)
Baneasa Airport
Bucharest, Romania
Tel. 33.00.30
TEXAS INTERNATIONAL AIRLINES (TI)
P.O. Box 12788
Houston, Texas 77017
Tel. 713—641-7100
THY (See Turk Hava Yollari)
TRANSAIR LIMITED (TZ)
Winnipeg International Airport
Winnipeg R3JOH7, Canada

Tel. 204-632-2811
TRANS-AUSTRALIA AIRLINES (TN)
50 Franklin St.
(P.O. Box 2806 AA)
Melbourne, C. 1, Victoria, Australia
Tel. 345-1333
TRANSBRASIL (S/A) LINHAS AEREAS (QD)
Aeroporto de Congonhas
Hangar da Transbrasil
Sao Paulo, Brazil
Tel. 267-7411
TRANSPORTES AEREOS NACIONALES (See TAN)
TRANS-PROVINCIAL AIRLINES LTD. (CD)
Box 280
Prince Rupert, B.C., Canada
Tel. 604-627-1341
TRANS WORLD AIRLINES, INC. (TW)
605 Third Avenue
New York, N.Y. 10016
Tel. 212-557-3000
TRINIDAD AND TOBAGO AIR SERVICES LTD. (HU)
Laughton Bldg.
37 Wrightson Road
Port of Spain, Trinidad
Tel. 62-52777
TUNIS AIR—Societe Tunisienne De L'Air (TU)
113 Avenue de la Liberte
Tunis, Tunisia
Tel. 288-100
TURK HAVA YOLLARI (TK)
Cumhuriyet Cad. 199-201
Harbiye-Istanbul, Turkey
Tel. 403013
TWA (See Trans World Airlines)
UNITED AIRLINES (UA)
P.O. Box 66100
Chicago, Illinois 60666

Tel. 312—952-4000
UNITED AIR (UE)
P.O. Box/Posbus 27010
Sunnyside 0132
Pretoria 0009, South Africa
Tel. 57-1181, 57-1183
U.T.A.—Union de Transportes Aeriens (UT)
50, Rue Arago 92
Puteaux, France
Tel. 775-22-33
VARIG, S.A.—Viacao Aerea Rio-Grandense (RG)
Ed. Varig. Av. Almte
Aeroporto Santos Dumont
Rio de Janeiro, Brazil
Tel. 52-3700
VASP—Viacao Aerea Sao Paulo, S.A. (VP)
04368 Edificio VASP
Aeroporto de Congonhas, 01000
Sao Paulo, Brazil
Tel. 267-7011
VIASA—Venezolana Internacional de Aviacion, S.A. (VA)
Ed. S. Caracas
(P.O. Box 6857)
Caracas, Venezuela
Tel. 811231
WAAC (See Nigeria Airways, Ltd.)
WEST COAST AIR SERVICES LTD. (MG)
518 Airport Road South
International Airport South
Vancouver, B.C., Canada
Tel. 604—278-8431
WESTERN AIRLINES, INC. (WA)
Los Angeles Airport
6060 Avion Drive
P.O. Box 92005
Airport Station
Los Angeles, California 90009

Tel. 213—646-2345
WIEN AIR ALASKA, INC. (WC)
4100 International Airport
Anchorage, Alaska 99502
Tel. 907—243-2400
**WINDWARD ISLAND AIRWAYS INTERNATIONAL
N.V. (WM)**
P.O. Box 288
St. Maarten, Netherland Antilles
Tel. 4230-4237
YUGOSLAV AIRLINES (JAT) (JU)
Bircaninova 1/III
11000 Belgrade, Yugoslavia
Tel. 26-227, 27-780
ZAMBIA AIRWAYS (QZ)
Haile Selassie Avenue
P.O. Box 272
Lusaka, Zambia
Tel. 53444

APPENDIX C
ABBREVIATIONS OF AIRLINE NAMES

This is an alphabetical list of the letter abbreviations used to identify airlines in timetables, travel brochures and airline tickets. Most scheduled airlines are included. Won't it be nice to know what you are reading!

CODE	AIRLINE
AA	AMERICAN AIRLINES
AC	AIR CANADA
AE	AIR CEYLON
AF	AIR FRANCE
AH	AIR ALGERIE
AI	AIR INDIA
AL	ALLEGHENY AIRLINES
AM	AEROMEXICO
AO	AVIACO
AP	ASPEN AIRWAYS, INC.
AQ	AIR ANGLIA LTD.
AR	AEROLINEAS ARGENTINAS
AS	ALASKA AIRLINES
AT	ROYAL AIR MAROC
AV	AVIANCA
AY	FINNAIR
AZ	ALITALIA
BA	BRITISH AIRWAYS
BD	BRITISH MIDLAND AIRWAYS
BE	BRITISH AIRWAYS

CODE	AIRLINE
BM	AERO TRASPORTI ITALIANI
BN	BRANIFF INTERNATIONAL AIRWAYS
BP	AIR BOTSWANA PTY. LTD.
BR	BRITISH CALEDONIAN AIRWAYS
BT	AIR MARTINIQUE (SATAIR)
BU	BRAATHENS S.A.F.E. AIRTRANSPORT
BW	B.W.I.A. INTERNATIONAL
CF	FAUCETT
CI	CHINA AIRLINES
CO	CONTINENTAL AIRLINES (AIR MICRONESIA)
CP	CP AIR
CU	CUBANA AIRLINES
CX	CATHAY PACIFIC AIRWAYS
CY	CYPRUS AIRWAYS
DA	DAN-AIR SERVICES, LTD.
DJ	AIR DJIBOUTI
DL	DELTA AIR LINES, INC.
DO	DOMINICANA DE AVIACION
DS	AIR SENEGAL
DW	DLT DEUTSCHE REGIONAL LUFTVERKEHRSGESELLSCHAFT MBH GERMAN DOMESTIC AIRLINES
DX	DANAIR
EA	EASTERN AIR LINES
EI	AER LINGUS (IRISH)
ET	ETHIOPIAN AIRLINES
EU	EMPRESA ECUATORIANA DE AVIACION
FG	ARIANA AFGHAN AIRLINES
FI	FLUGFELAG-ICELANDAIR
FJ	AIR PACIFIC
FL	FRONTIER AIRLINES
FZ	MALDIVES INTERNATIONAL AIRLINES
GA	GARUDA INDONESIAN AIRWAYS
GB	AIR INTER GABON
GF	GULF AIR
GH	GHANA AIRWAYS

CODE	AIRLINE
GJ	ANSETT AIRLINES OF SOUTH AUSTRALIA
GK	LAKER AIRWAYS, LTD.
GL	GREENLANDAIR
GN	AIR GABON
GU	AVIATECA
GY	GUYANA AIRWAYS
HA	HAWAIIAN AIRLINES
HB	AIR MELANESIAE
HN	NLM-DUTCH AIRLINES
HU	TRINIDAD AND TOBAGO AIR SERVICES, LTD.
IA	IRAQI AIRWAYS
IB	IBERIA
IC	INDIAN AIRLINES
IF	INTERFLUG
IG	ALISARDA
IH	ITAVIA
IJ	TOURAINE AIR TRANSPORT
IO	AIR PARIS
IQ	CARIBBEAN AIRWAYS
IR	IRAN NATIONAL AIRLINES
IS	LUXAVIA
IT	AIR INTER
IY	YEMEN AIRWAYS CORP.
IZ	ARKIA-ISRAEL INLAND AIRLINES LTD.
JL	JAPAN AIR LINES COMPANY, LTD.
JM	AIR JAMAICA LTD.
JR	DELTA AIR
JU	YUGOSLAV AIRLINES—JAT
KE	KOREAN AIR LINES
KL	KLM—ROYAL DUTCH AIRLINES
KM	AIR MALTA COMPANY, LTD.— AIR MALTA
KO	KODIAK WESTERN ALASKA AIRLINES
KQ	KENYA AIRWAYS
KR	KAR-AIR
KU	KUWAIT AIRWAYS
LA	LAN CHILE

CODE	AIRLINE
LG	LUXAIR—LUXEMBOURG AIRLINES
LH	LUFTHANSA GERMAN AIRLINES
LJ	SIERRA LEONE AIRWAYS
LL	ICELANDIC AIRLINES
LN	LIBYAN ARAB AIRLINES
LO	LOT—POLISH AIRLINES
LP	AIR ALPES
LV	LAV—LINEA AEROPOSTAL VENEZOLANA
LX	AIR LANGUEDOC
LY	EL AL ISRAEL AIRLINES
LZ	BULGARIAN AIRLINES—BALKAN
MA	MALEV—HUNGARIAN AIRLINES
MD	AIR MADAGASCAR
ME	MIDDLE EAST AIRLINES/AIRLIBAN
MG	WEST COAST AIR SERVICES, LTD.
MH	MALAYSIAN AIRLINE SYSTEM
MK	AIR MAURITIUS
MR	AIR MAURITANIE
MS	EGYPTAIR
MX	MEXICANA DE AVIACION
MY	AIR MALI
NA	NATIONAL AIRLINES
NC	NORTH CENTRAL AIRLINES
ND	NORDAIR
NE	AIR NEW ENGLAND
NH	ALL NIPPON
NL	AIR LIBERIA, INC.
NU	SOUTHWEST AIRLINES CO., INC.
NW	NORTHWEST ORIENT AIRLINES, INC.
NY	NEW YORK AIRWAYS
NZ	AIR NEW ZEALAND—DOMESTIC
OA	OLYMPIC AIRWAYS
OD	AEROCONDOR
OG	AIR GUADELOUPE
OI	TRANSPORTES AEREOS NACIONALES LTDA.-TANA
OK	CZECHOSLOVAK AIRLINES
OM	AIR MONGOL—MIAT

CODE	AIRLINE
OP	AIR PANAMA INTERNACIONAL
OS	AUSTRIAN AIRLINES
OZ	OZARK AIR LINES
PA	PAN AMERICAN WORLD AIRWAYS
PB	AIR BURUNDI
PC	FIJI AIR
PG	PACIFIC COASTAL AIRLINES, LTD.
PH	POLYNESIAN AIRLINES
PI	PIEDMONT AVIATION
PK	PAKISTAN INTERNATIONAL
PL	AEROPERU
PR	PHILIPPINE AIRLINES
PW	PACIFIC WESTERN AIRLINES
PY	SURINAM AIRWAYS
PZ	LAP—LINEAS AEREAS PARAGUAYAS
QB	QUEBECAIR INC.
QC	AIR ZAIRE
QE	AIR TAHITI
QF	QANTAS AIRWAYS LTD.
QM	AIR MALAWI
QZ	ZAMBIA AIRWAYS
RA	ROYAL NEPAL AIRLINES
RB	SYRIAN ARAB AIRLINES
RG	VARIG, S.A.
RH	AIR RHODESIA
RI	EASTERN AIRLINES
RJ	ALIA-ROYAL JORDANIAN AIRLINES
RK	AIR AFRIQUE
RN	ROYAL AIR INTER
RO	TAROM—ROMANIAN AIR TRANSPORT
RQ	GREAT CHINA AIRLINES
RW	HUGHES AIRWEST
SA	SOUTH AFRICAN AIRWAYS
SD	SUDAN AIRWAYS
SH	SAHSA—SERVICIO AEREO DE HONDURAS, S.A.
SK	SAS—SCANDINAVIAN AIRLINES
SN	SABENA—BELGIAN AIRLINES

CODE	AIRLINE
SO	SOUTHERN AIRWAYS
SP	SATA
SQ	SINGAPORE AIRLINES
SR	SWISSAIR
SU	AEROFLOT SOVIET AIRLINES
SV	SAUDI ARABIAN AIRLINES
SY	AIR ALSACE
TA	TACA INTERNATIONAL
TC	AIR TANZANIA CORPORATION
TE	AIR NEW ZEALAND—INTERNATIONAL
TI	TEXAS INTERNATIONAL AIRLINES, INC.
TK	TURK HAVA YOLLARI
TM	DETA
TN	TRANS-AUSTRALIA AIRLINES
TP	TAP
TS	ALOHA AIRLINES
TU	TUNIS AIR
TW	TRANS WORLD AIRLINES
TY	AIR CALEDONIE
TZ	TRANSAIR LIMITED
UA	UNITED AIRLINES
UB	BURMA AIRWAYS CORP.
UI	FLUGFELAG NORDURLANDS H.F.
UK	BRITISH ISLAND AIRWAYS, LTD.
UN	NEW ENGLAND AIRWAYS PTY. LTD.
UP	BAHAMASAIR
UY	CAMEROON AIRLINES
UZ	AIR ROUERGUE
VA	VIASA
VT	AIR POLYNESIE
VU	AIR IVOIRE
WT	NIGERIA AIRWAYS, LTD.
WW	TRANS-WEST
XZ	AIR TASMANIA PTY. LTD.
ZV	AIR MIDWEST
ZX	AIR WEST AIRLINES, LTD.

APPENDIX D
AIRPORT/CITY CODES IN THE U.S. AND ABROAD

All baggage tags are marked with airport /city codes. If you do not know what the correct code is for your destination, there is no way to make sure your bags have been correctly routed. With the list provided below you can keep your eye out for such errors. The list covers nearly every airport in the U.S. and many around the world.

AIRPORT CODES/ALPHABETICAL ORDER BY CITY

A

ABR	ABERDEEN, SD
ABJ	ABIDJAN, IVORY COAST
ABI	ABILENE, TX
ACA	ACAPULCO, MEXICO
ADD	ADDIS ABABA, ETHIOPIA
CAK	AKRON/CANTON, OH
ALM	ALAMOGORDO, NM
ALS	ALAMOSA, CO
XAL	ALAMOS, MEXICO
ABY	ALBANY, GA
ALB	ALBANY, NY
ABQ	ALBUQUERQUE, NM
AXN	ALEXANDRIA, MN
ESF	ALEXANDRIA, LA
ALG	ALGIERS, ALGERIA

ABE	ALLENTOWN, PA
AIA	ALLIANCE, NB
AOO	ALTOONA, PA
AXS	ALTUS, OK
AMA	AMARILLO, TX
AMS	AMSTERDAM, NETHERLANDS
ANC	ANCHORAGE, AK
ASD	ANDROS TOWN, BAHAMAS
AXA	ANGUILLA, WEST INDIES
ESB	ANKARA, TURKEY
ANU	ANTIGUA, WEST INDIES
ATW	APPLETON, WI
AUA	ARUBA, NETH. ANTILLES
ARX	ASBURY PARK, NJ
AVL	ASHEVILLE, NC
ASE	ASPEN, CO
ASU	ASUNCION, PARAGUAY
AHN	ATHENS, GA
ATH	ATHENS, GREECE
ATO	ATHENS, OH
AIY	ATLANTIC CITY, NJ
ATL	ATLANTA, GA
AKL	AUCKLAND, NEW ZEALAND
AGS	AUGUSTA, GA
AUG	AUGUSTA, ME
AUS	AUSTIN, TX

B

BGW	BAGHDAD, IRAQ
BAH	BAHRAIN, BAHRAIN
BFL	BAKERSFIELD, CA
BAL	BALTIMORE, MD
BKK	BANGKOK, THAILAND
BGR	BANGOR, ME
BHB	BAR HARBOR, ME
BGI	BARBADOS, BARBADOS
BCN	BARCELONA, SPAIN
BSL	BASEL, SWITZERLAND
BTR	BATON ROUGE, LA

BTL	BATTLE CREEK, MI
BPT	BEAUMONT/PT. ARTHUR, TX
BKW	BECKLEY, WV
BED	BEDFORD, MA
BEY	BEIRUT, LEBANON
BFS	BELFAST, N. IRELAND
BEG	BELGRADE, YUGOSLAVIA
BLI	BELLINGHAM, WA
JVL	BELOIT/JANESVILLE, WI
BJI	BEMIDJI, MN
BEN	BENGASI, LIBYA
BEH	BENTON HARBOR, MI
TXL	BERLIN, GERMANY—WEST
BDA	BERMUDA, ATLANTIC OCEAN
BIL	BILLINGS, MT
BIM	BIMINI, BAHAMAS
NSB	BIMINI, BAHAMAS—N. SEAPLANE
BGM	BINGHAMTON, NY
BHM	BIRMINGHAM, AL
BIS	BISMARCK, ND
BID	BLOCK ISLAND, RI
BMG	BLOOMINGTON, IN
BMI	BLOOMINGTON, IL
BLH	BLYTHE, CA
BGR	BANGOR, ME
BOG	BOGOTA, COLOMBIA
BOI	BOISE, ID
BOM	BOMBAY, INDIA
BOS	BOSTON, MA
BWG	BOWLING GREEN, KY
BFD	BRADFORD, PA
BRD	BRAINERD, MN
BSB	BRASILIA, BRAZIL
BDR	BRIDGEPORT, CT
BKX	BROOKINGS, SD
BRO	BROWNSVILLE, TX
BRU	BRUSSELS, BELGIUM
BUH	BUCHAREST, ROMANIA
BUD	BUDAPEST, HUNGARY

EZE	BUENOS AIRES, ARG—EZEIZA ARPT.
BUF	BUFFALO, NY
BUR	BURBANK, CA
BRL	BURLINGTON, IA
BTV	BURLINGTON, VT
BTM	BUTTE, MT

C

CAD	CADILLAC, MI
CAI	CAIRO, ARAB REP. OF EGYPT
CCU	CALCUTTA, INDIA
YYC	CALGARY, ALTA., CANADA
CUN	CANCUN, MEXICO
CAP	CAP HAITIEN, HAITI
CGI	CAPE GIRARDEAU, MO
WWD	CAPE MAY, NJ
CCS	CARACAS, VENEZUELA
MDH	CARBONDALE, IL
CNM	CARLSBAD, NM
CSN	CARSON CITY, NV
CAS	CASABLANCA, MOROCCO—NOUASSEUR
CPR	CASPER, WY
AVX	CATALINA IS., CA—AVALON BAY
TWH	CATALINA IS., CA
MSV	CATSKILL MTS/SULLIVAN CO NY
CYA	CAYES, HAITI
CYB	CAYMAN BRAC, WEST INDIES
CID	CEDAR RAPIDS/IOWA CITY, IA
CDR	CHADRON, NB
CMI	CHAMPAIGN, IL
STT	CHARLOTTE AMALIE, ST. THOMAS
CHO	CHARLOTTESVILLE, VA
CHS	CHARLESTON, WV
CLT	CHARLOTTE, NC
CRW	CHARLESTON, WV
CHA	CHATTANOOGA, TN
CYS	CHEYENNE, WY
ORD	CHICAGO, IL—O'HARE ARPT.

CUU	CHIHUAHUA, MEXICO
CFG	CIENFUEGOS, CUBA
CVG	CINCINNATI, OH
CKB	CLARKSBURG, WV
BKL	CLEVELAND, OHIO—LAKEFRONT ARPT.
CLE	CLEVELAND, OH
CWI	CLINTON, IA
CVN	CLOVIS, NM
CLL	COLLEGE STATION, TX
CGN	COLOGNE-DUSSELDORF, GERMANY
COS	COLORADO SPRGS, CO
CAE	COLUMBIA, SC
CDA	COLUMBIA, CA
COU	COLUMBIA, MO
CSG	COLUMBUS, GA
CMH	COLUMBUS, OH
GTR	COLUMBUS, MI
OLU	COLUMBUS, NB
CON	CONCORD, NH
CPH	COPENHAGEN, DENMARK
CRP	CORPUS CHRISTI, TX
CVO	CORVALLIS, OR
CZM	COZUMEL, MEXICO
CEC	CRESCENT CITY, CA
CSE	CRESTED BUTTE, CO
CKD	CROOKED CREEK, AK
CUR	CURACAO, NETH. ANTILLES

D

DKR	DAKAR, SENEGAL
DFW	DALLAS/FT. WORTH, TX
DAM	DAMASCUS, SYRIA
DNV	DANVILLE, IL
DAR	DAR ES SALAAM, TANZANIA
DAB	DAYTONA BEACH, FL
DAY	DAYTON, OH
DEO	DEARBORN, MI
DEC	DECATUR, IL
DRT	DEL RIO, TX

DEL	DELHI, INDIA
DEN	DENVER, CO
DSM	DES MOINES, IA
DET	DETROIT, MI—CITY ARPT.
DTL	DETROIT LAKES, MN
DTT	DETROIT, MI
DTW	DETROIT, MI—METRO ARPT.
DVL	DEVILS LAKE, ND
DDC	DODGE CITY, KA
DUB	DUBLIN, IRELAND
DBQ	DUBUQUE, IA
DLH	DULUTH, MN
DGO	DURANGO, MEXICO
DRO	DURANGO, CO
DUS	DUSSELDORF, GERMANY

E

HTO	EAST HAMPTON, NY
EAU	EAU CLAIRE, WI
YEG	EDMONTON, ALBERTA, CANADA
EIP	EL CENTRO, CA
ELP	EL PASO, TX
EKI	ELKHART, IN
EKO	ELKO, NV
ELM	ELMIRA, NY
ELY	ELY, NV
EMP	EMPORIA, KS
WDG	ENID, OK
EBB	ENTEBBE, UGANDA
ERI	ERIE, PA
ESC	ESCANABA, MI
EUG	EUGENE, OR
ACV	EUREKA/ARCATA, CA
EVV	EVANSVILLE, IN

F

FAI	FAIRBANKS, AK
FAR	FARGO, ND

FMN	FARMINGTON, NM
FRG	FARMINGDALE, NY
FAY	FAYETTEVILLE, NC
FYV	FAYETTEVILLE, AR
FLG	FLAGSTAFF, AZ
FNT	FLINT, MI
FDF	FT. DE FRANCE, MARTINIQUE
FMS	FT. MADISON, IA
FMY	FT. MYERS, FL
FTC	FT. COLLINS, CO
FFT	FRANKFORT, KY
FRA	FRANKFURT, REP. OF GERMANY
FPO	FREEPORT, BAHAMAS
FAT	FRESNO, CA
FOD	FT. DODGE, IA
FLL	FT. LAUDERDALE, FL
TBN	FT. LEONARD WOOD, MO
FSM	FT. SMITH, AR
FWA	FT. WAYNE, IN
FUL	FULLERTON, CA

G

GNV	GAINESVILLE, FL
GBG	GALESBURG, IL
GQQ	GALION, OH
GUP	GALLUP, NM
GLS	GALVESTON, TX
YQX	GANDER, NFLD., CANADA
GCK	GARDEN CITY, KS
GVA	GENEVA, SWITZERLAND
GED	GEORGETOWN, DE
GGT	GEORGE TOWN, BAHAMAS
GCC	GILLETTE, WY
PIK	GLASGOW, SCOT.—PRESTWICK ARPT.
GLD	GOODLAND, KS
YYR	GOOSE BAY, NFLD., CANADA
GEO	GEORGETOWN, GUYANA
GNY	GRANBY, CO
GCM	GRAND CAYMAN, WEST INDIES

GCN	GRAND CANYON, AZ
ZGF	GRAND FORKS, B.C., CANADA
GFK	GRAND FORKS, ND
GRI	GRAND ISLAND, NB
GJT	GRAND JUNCTION, CO
YQU	GRANDE PRAIRIE, ALTA., CANADA
GPZ	GRAND RAPIDS, MN
GRR	GRAND RAPIDS, MI
GDT	GRAND TURK, B.W.I.
GBD	GREAT BEND, KS
GTF	GREAT FALLS, MT
GHC	GREAT HARBOUR CAY, BAHAMAS
GRB	GREEN BAY, WI
GSO	GREENSBORO/HIGH POINT, NC
GSP	GREENVILLE/SPARTANBURG SC
LWB	GREENBRIER, WV
GND	GRENADA, WINDWARD IS.
GDL	GUADALAJARA, MEXICO
GUM	GUAM ISLAND, MARINA IS.
GAO	GUANTANAMO, CUBA
GUA	GUATEMALA CITY, GUATEMALA
GYM	GUAYMAS, MEXICO
GPT	GULFPORT/BILOXI, MS
GUC	GUNNISON, CO

H

HGR	HAGERSTOWN, MD
YHZ	HALIFAX, N.S., CANADA
HAM	HAMBURG, REP. OF GERMANY
YHM	HAMILTON, ONT., CANADA
HAJ	HANNOVER, GERMANY
HRL	HARLINGEN, TX
MDT	HARRISBURG, PA
BDL	HARTFORD CT/SPRINGFIELD, MA
HSI	HASTINGS, NB
HNC	HATTERAS, NC
HAV	HAVANA, CUBA
HVR	HAVRE, MT

HYS	HAYS, KS
HLN	HELENA, MT
HEL	HELSINKI, FINLAND
HMO	HERMOSILLO, MEXICO
HIB	HIBBING, MN
ITO	HILO, HAWAII, HAWAII
HHH	HILTON HEAD ISLAND, SC
HOM	HOMER, AK
HKG	HONG KONG, HONG KONG
HNL	HONOLULU, OAHU, HI
HOT	HOT SPRINGS, AR
HSP	HOT SPRINGS, VA
HOU	HOUSTON, TX—HOBBY ARPT.
IAH	HOUSTON, TX
HUS	HUGHES, AK
HTS	HUNTINGTON, WV
HON	HURON, SD
HUT	HUTCHINSON, KS
HYA	HYANNIS, MA

I

IDA	IDAHO FALLS, ID
YGR	ILES DE MADELEINE, QUE., CANADA
IND	INDIANAPOLIS, IN
INL	INT'L FALLS, MN
IMT	IRON MOUNTAIN, MI
IWD	IRONWOOD, MI
ISP	ISLIP, NY
IST	ISTANBUL, TURKEY
ITH	ITHACA, NY

J

JXN	JACKSON, MI
MKL	JACKSON, TN
JAC	JACKSON, WY
JAN	JACKSON/VICKSBURG, MS
JAX	JACKSONVILLE, FL
IJX	JACKSONVILLE, IL

OAJ	JACKSONVILLE, NC
HLP	JAKARTA, INDONESIA
JHW	JAMESTOWN, NY
JMS	JAMESTOWN, ND
JED	JEDDAH, SAUDI ARABIA
JEF	JEFFERSON CITY, MO
NNB	JOHANNESBURG, SOUTH AFRICA
JST	JOHNSTOWN, PA
JBR	JONESBORO, AR
JLN	JOPLIN, MO
JNU	JUNEAU, AK

K

AZO	KALAMAZOO, MI
MCI	KANSAS CITY, MO
KHI	KARACHI, PAKISTAN
ZKE	KASHECHEWAN, ONT., CANADA
EAR	KEARNEY, NB
EOK	KEOKUK, IA
KTN	KETCHIKAN, AK
EYW	KEY WEST, FL
KRT	KHARTOUM, SUDAN
IGM	KINGMAN, AZ
KIN	KINGSTON, JAMAICA
FIH	KINSHASA, ZAIRE
IRK	KIRKSVILLE, MO
LMT	KLAMATH FALLS, OR
TYS	KNOXVILLE, TN
ADQ	KODIAK, AK—KODIAK ARPT.
OKK	KOKOMO, IN
KOA	KONA, HAWAII, HI
KUL	KUALA LUMPUR, MALAYSIA
KWI	KUWAIT, KUWAIT

L

LSE	LA CROSSE, WI
LAF	LAFAYETTE, IN
LFT	LAFAYETTE, LA
LOS	LAGOS, NIGERIA

LCH	LAKE CHARLES, LA
LHU	LAKE HAVASU CITY, AZ
AIZ	LAKE OF THE OZARKS, MO
TVL	LAKE TAHOE, CA
LAA	LAMAR, CO
LNY	LANAI CITY, LANAI, HI
LNS	LANCASTER, PA
LAN	LANSING, MI
LAP	LA PAZ, MEXICO
LPB	LA PAZ, BOLIVIA
LPO	LA PORTE, IN
LAR	LARAMIE, WY
LRD	LAREDO, TX
LRU	LAS CRUCES, NM
LAS	LAS VEGAS, NV
PIB	LAUREL/HATTIESBURG, MS
LWC	LAWRENCE, KS
LAW	LAWTON, OK
LXV	LEADVILLE, CO
LEB	LEBANON, NH
LED	LENINGRAD, USSR
LWS	LEWISTON, ID
LEW	LEWISTON, ME
LMT	LEWISTOWN, MT
LEX	LEXINGTON/FRANKFORT, KY
LXN	LEXINGTON, NB
LBL	LIBERAL, KS
LIM	LIMA, PERU
LNK	LINCOLN, NB
LIS	LISBON, PORTUGAL
LIT	LITTLE ROCK, AR
LGU	LOGAN, UT
LGW	LONDON, ENG—GATWICK ARPT.
LHR	LONDON, ENG—HEATHROW ARPT.
LOZ	LONDON, KY
YXU	LONDON, ONT., CANADA
LGB	LONG BEACH, CA
GGG	LONGVIEW, TX
LAM	LOS ALAMOS, NM

LAX	LOS ANGELES, CA
SDF	LOUISVILLE, KY
LOL	LOVELOCK, NV
LBB	LUBBOCK, TX
LFK	LUFKIN, TX
LYH	LYNCHBURG, VA

M

MQB	MACOMB, IL
MCN	MACON, GA
MSN	MADISON, WI
MDJ	MADRAS, OR
MAD	MADRID, SPAIN
AGP	MALAGA, SPAIN
MAW	MALDEN, MO
MMH	MAMMOTH LAKES, CA
MGA	MANAGUA, NICARAGUA
MNZ	MANASSAS, VA
MAO	MANAUS, BRAZIL
MHT	MANCHESTER, NH
MDL	MANDALAY, BURMA
MAY	MANGROVE CAY, BAHAMAS
MHK	MANHATTAN, KS
MNL	MANILA, PHILIPPINES
MBL	MANISTEE, MI
MTW	MANITOWOC, WI
MKT	MANKATO, MN
MFD	MANSFIELD, OH
MZO	MANZANILLO, CUBA
ZLO	MANZANILLO, MEXICO
MAR	MARACAIBO, VENEZUELA
MTH	MARATHON, FL
MRK	MARCO ISLAND, FL
GBJ	MARIE GALANTE, FR. ANTILLES
MWA	MARION, IL
MQT	MARQUETTE, MI
MRS	MARSEILLES, FRANCE
MML	MARSHALL, MN
MVY	MARTHA'S VINEYARD, MA

MCW	MASON CITY, IA
MSS	MASSENA, NY
MAM	MATAMOROS, MEXICO
MTO	MATTOON, IL
MZT	MAZATLAN, MEXICO
MLC	MC ALESTER, OK
MFE	MC ALLEN, TX
MCK	MC COOK, NB
MCL	MC KINLEY NAT'L PK., AK
MFR	MEDFORD, OR
YXH	MEDICINE HAT, ALTA., CANADA
MEL	MELBOURNE, AUSTRALIA
MLB	MELBOURNE, FL
MEM	MEMPHIS, TN
MNM	MENOMINEE, MI
MCE	MERCED, CA
MEI	MERIDIAN, MS
MID	MERIDA, MEXICO
MXL	MEXICALI, MEXICO
MEX	MEXICO CITY, MEXICO
MIA	MIAMI, FL
MGC	MICHIGAN CITY, IN
MAF	MIDLAND/ODESSA, TX
MDY	MIDWAY ISLAND, PACIFIC
MXP	MILAN, ITALY—MALPENSO ARPT.
MLS	MILES CITY, MT
MLF	MILFORD, UT
MIV	MILLVILLE, NJ
MKE	MILWAUKEE, WI
MSP	MINNEAPOLIS/ST. PAUL, MN
MOT	MINOT, ND
MSO	MISSOULA, MT
MHE	MITCHELL, SD
CNY	MOAB, UT
MOB	MOBILE AL/PASCAGOULA, MS
MOD	MODESTO, CA
MHV	MOJAVE, CA
MLI	MOLINE, IL
MLU	MONROE, LA

ROB	MONROVIA, LIBERIA
MTP	MONTAUK POINT, NY
MBJ	MONTEGO BAY, JAMAICA
MRY	MONTEREY, CA
MTY	MONTERREY, MEXICO
MVD	MONTEVIDEO, URUGUAY
MGM	MONTGOMERY, AL
MXC	MONTICELLO, UT
MPV	MONTPELIER, VT
MTJ	MONTROSE, CO
YUL	MONTREAL, QUE., CANADA
MNI	MONTSERRAT, MONTSERRAT
MGW	MORGANTOWN, WV
PTN	MORGAN CITY/PATTERSON, LA
SVO	MOSCOW, U.S.S.R.—SHEREMETYEVO ARPT.
MGR	MOULTRIE/THOMASVILLE, GA
MVN	MOUNT VERNON, IL
MVW	MOUNT VERNON, WA
MIE	MUNCIE, IN
MUC	MUNICH, REP. OF GERMANY
MSL	MUSCLE SHOALS, AL
MKG	MUSKEGON, MI
MYR	MYRTLE BEACH, SC

N

OCH	NACOGDOCHES, TX
NAN	NADI, FIJI
NBO	NAIROBI, KENYA
ZNU	NAMU, B.C., CANADA
ACK	NANTUCKET, MA
APC	NAPA, CA
APF	NAPLES, FL
NAP	NAPLES, ITALY
BNA	NASHVILLE, TN
NAS	NASSAU, BAHAMAS
HEZ	NATCHEZ, MS
NEG	NEGRIL, JAMAICA
EWR	NEWARK, NJ

EWB	NEW BEDFORD, MA
HVN	NEW HAVEN, CT
GON	NEW LONDON, CT
MSY	NEW ORLEANS, LA
NPT	NEWPORT, RI
PHF	NEWPORT NEWS, VA
JFK	NEW YORK, NY—KENNEDY INT'L ARPT.
LGA	NEW YORK, NY—LA GUARDIA ARPT.
NYC	NEW YORK, NY—NEWARK, NJ
NCE	NICE, FRANCE
OME	NOME, AK
OFK	NORFOLK, NB
ORF	NORFOLK, VA
NMC	NORMAN'S CAY, BAHAMAS
ELH	NORTH ELEUTHERA, BAHAMAS
LBF	NORTH PLATTE, NB
NLD	NUEVO LAREDO, MEXICO
NUE	NUREMBERG, GERMANY

O

OAK	OAKLAND, CA
OAX	OAXACA, MEXICO
OCE	OCEAN CITY, MD
OCJ	OCHO RIOS, JAMAICA
AHA	OKINAWA ISLAND, JAPAN
OKC	OKLAHOMA CITY, OK
OLM	OLYMPIA, WA
OMA	OMAHA, NB
ONH	ONEONTA, NY
ONO	ONTARIO, OR
ONT	ONTARIO, CA
SNA	ORANGE COUNTY, CA
MCO	ORLANDO, FL
OSB	OSAGE BEACH, MO
OSA	OSAKA, JAPAN
OSH	OSHKOSH, WI
OSL	OSLO, NORWAY

YOW	OTTAWA, ONT., CANADA
OTM	OTTUMWA, IA
OWB	OWENSBORO, KY
OXR	OXNARD, CA

P

PAH	PADUCAH, KY
PPG	PAGO PAGO, SAMOA
PSP	PALM SPRINGS, CA
PFN	PANAMA CITY, FL
PTY	PANAMA CITY, PANAMA REP.
PPT	PAPEETE, TAHITI
CDG	PARIS, FRANCE—CHARLES DE GAULLE ARPT.
LBG	PARIS, FRANCE—LE BOURGET ARPT.
ORY	PARIS, FRANCE—ORLY ARPT.
PRX	PARIS, TX
PKB	PARKERSBURG, WV
PPF	PARSONS, KS
PRB	PASO ROBLES, CA
PLN	PELLSTON, MI
PNS	PENSACOLA, FL
PIA	PEORIA, IL
PER	PERTH, W. AUSTRALIA
YPQ	PETERBOROUGH, ONT., CANADA
PHL	PHILADELPHIA, PA/WILM'TON DEL.
PSB	PHILIPSBURG, PA
PHX	PHOENIX, AZ
PIR	PIERRE, SD
PBF	PINE BLUFF, AR
SOP	PINEHURST, NC
PSA	PISA, ITALY
PIT	PITTSBURGH, PA
PSF	PITTSFIELD, MA
PIH	POCATELLO, ID
PTP	POINTE A PITRE, GUADELOUPE
PNC	PONCA CITY, OK
PSE	PONCE, PR

POF	POPLAR BLUFF, MO
CLM	PORT ANGELES, WA
POT	PORT ANTONIO, JAMAICA
PAP	PORT AU PRINCE, HAITI
PDX	PORTLAND, OR
PWM	PORTLAND, ME
POS	PORT OF SPAIN, TRIN.
POU	POUGHKEEPSIE, NY
PRG	PRAGUE, CZECHOSLOVAKIA
PRC	PRESCOTT, AZ
PCT	PRINCETON, NJ
YPA	PRINCE ALBERT, SASK., CANADA
YXS	PRINCE GEORGE, B.C., CANADA
ZSW	PRINCE RUPERT, B.C.—SEAL COVE
YPR	PRINCE RUPERT, B.C., CANADA
PVD	PROVIDENCE, RI
PVC	PROVINCETOWN, MA
PUD	PRUDHOE BAY/SAG RIV, AK
PUB	PUEBLO, CO
PVR	PUERTO VALLARTA, MEXICO
PUW	PULLMAN, WA

Q

YQB	QUEBEC, QUE., CANADA
UIN	QUINCY, IL
UIO	QUITO, ECUADOR

R

RBA	RABAT, MOROCCO
RDU	RALEIGH/DURHAM, NC
RGN	RANGOON, BURMA
RAP	RAPID CITY, SD
RWL	RAWLINS, WY
RDG	READING, PA
RDD	REDDING, CA
RNO	RENO, NV
REX	REYNOSA, MEXICO
RHI	RHINELANDER, WI
RIC	RICHMOND, VA

GIG   RIO DE JANEIRO, BRA—GALEAC ARPT.
RAL   RIVERSIDE, CA
RIW   RIVERTON, WY
ROA   ROANOKE, VA
RST   ROCHESTER, MN
ROC   ROCHESTER, NY
RFD   ROCKFORD, IL
RKD   ROCKLAND, ME
RLA   ROLLA, MO
CIA   ROME, ITALY—CIAMPINO ARPT.
FCO   ROME, ITALY—LEONARDO DA VINCI ARPT.
ROW   ROSWELL, NM
RUI   RUIDOSO, NM
RUT   RUTLAND, VT

S

SAB   SABA, NETH. ANTILLES
SMF   SACRAMENTO, CA
MBS   SAGINAW, MI
SGW   SAGINAW, AK
STX   ST. CROIX, VIRGIN IS.
YSJ   ST. JOHN, N.B., CANADA
SJF   ST. JOHN, VIRGIN IS.
YYT   ST. JOHNS, NFLD., CANADA
SKB   ST. KITTS, BRITISH WEST INDIES
STL   ST. LOUIS, MO
SXM   ST. MAARTEN, NETH. ANTILLES
PIE   ST. PETERSBURG, FL
SSI   ST. SIMONS ISLAND, GA
SPB   ST. THOMAS, VIRGIN IS—SEAPLANE BASE
STT   ST. THOMAS, VIRGIN IS.
SLE   SALEM, OR
SLN   SALINA, KS
SLC   SALT LAKE CITY, UT
SAQ   SAN ANDROS, BAHAMAS
SJT   SAN ANGELO, TX

SAT	SAN ANTONIO, TX
SAN	SAN DIEGO, CA
SFO	SAN FRANCISCO/OAKLAND, CA
SJC	SAN JOSE, CA
SJO	SAN JOSE, COSTA RICA
SIG	SAN JUAN, PR—ISLA GRANDE ARPT.
SJU	SAN JUAN, PR
SBP	SAN LUIS OBISPO, CA
SPQ	SAN PEDRO, CA
ZSA	SAN SALVADOR, BAHAMAS
SBA	SANTA BARBARA, CA
SAF	SANTA FE, NM
SNU	SANTA CLARA, CUBA
SMA	SANTA MARIA, AZORES
STS	SANTA ROSA, CA
SCL	SANTIAGO, CHILE
SCU	SANTIAGO, CUBA
STI	SANTIAGO, DOM. REP.
SDQ	SANTO DOMINGO, DOM. REP.
CGH	SAO PAULO, BRA.—CONGONHAS ARPT.
VCP	SAO PAULO, BRA—VIRACOPOS ARPT.
SLK	SARANAC LAKE, NY
SRQ	SARASOTA/BRADENTON, FL
YXE	SASKATOON, SASK., CANADA
SSM	SAULT STE MARIE, MI
SAV	SAVANNAH, GA
BFF	SCOTTSBLUFF, NB
SEA	SEATTLE/TACOMA, WA
DMO	SEDALIA, MO
SEL	SEOUL, SOUTH KOREA
SWD	SEWARD, AK
SHA	SHANGHAI, CHINA
SNN	SHANNON, IRELAND
SBM	SHEBOYGAN, WI
SHR	SHERIDAN, WY
SHV	SHREVEPORT, LA

SNY	SIDNEY, NB
SVC	SILVER CITY, NM
SIN	SINGAPORE, SINGAPORE
SUX	SIOUX CITY, IA
FSD	SIOUX FALLS, SD
SOF	SOFIA, RUMANIA
TZN	SOUTH ANDROS, BAHAMAS
SBN	SOUTH BEND, IN
GEG	SPOKANE, WA
SGF	SPRINGFIELD, MO
SPI	SPRINGFIELD, IL
VSF	SPRINGFIELD, VT
SCE	STATE COLLEGE, PA
SHD	STAUNTON, VA
HDN	STEAMBOAT SPRINGS, CO
STK	STERLING, CO
ARN	STOCKHOLM, SWEDEN—ARLANDO ARPT.
SCK	STOCKTON, CA
SUE	STURGEON BAY, WI
STR	STUTTGART, GERMANY
SUM	SUMTER, SC
SUN	SUN VALLEY, ID
SYD	SYDNEY, N.S.W. AUSTRALIA
SYR	SYRACUSE, NY

T

TPE	TAIPEI, TAIWAN
TLH	TALLAHASSEE, FL
TPA	TAMPA, FL
TAM	TAMPICO, MEXICO
THR	TEHRAN, IRAN
TLV	TEL AVIV—JAFFA, ISRAEL
TPL	TEMPLE, TX
TCI	TENERIFE, CANARY IS.
HUG	TERRE HAUTE, IN
TXK	TEXARKANA, AR
YQT	THUNDER BAY, ONT., CANADA
TIJ	TIJUANA, MEXICO

TAB	TOBAGO, TRINIDAD & TOBAGO
HND	TOKYO, JAPAN—HANEDO ARPT.
NRT	TOKYO, JAPAN—NARITA ARPT.
TOL	TOLEDO, OH
FOE	TOPEKA, KS
YYZ	TORONTO, ONT., CANADA
TRC	TORREON, MEXICO
TVC	TRAVERSE CITY, MI
TCB	TREASURE CAY, BAHAMAS
TTN	TRENTON, NJ
TRI	TRI-CITY AIRPORT, TN
TIP	TRIPOLI, LIBYA
TUS	TUCSON, AZ
TUL	TULSA, OK
TUN	TUNIS, TUNISIA
TUP	TUPELO, MS
TRN	TURIN, ITALY
TCL	TUSCALOOSA, AL
TGE	TUSKEGEE, AL
TWF	TWIN FALLS, ID
TYR	TYLER, TX

U

UOX	UNIVERSITY, MS
UCA	UTICA, NY

V

EGE	VAIL/EAGLE, CO
VDZ	VALDEZ, AK
VLD	VALDOSTA, GA
VPZ	VALPARAISO, IN
YVR	VANCOUVER, B.C., CANADA
VER	VERACRUZ, MEXICO
VCT	VICTORIA, TX
YYJ	VICTORIA, B.C., CANADA
VIE	VIENNA, AUSTRIA
VSA	VILLAHERMOSA, MEXICO
VIJ	VIRGIN GORDA, BR. VIRGIN IS.

W

ACT	WACO, TX
ALW	WALLA WALLA, WA
WAW	WARSAW, POLAND
DCA	WASHINGTON, DC—NATIONAL ARPT.
IAD	WASHINGTON, DC—DULLES ARPT.
ALO	WATERLOO, IA
CWA	WAUSAU, WIS—CENTRAL WIS ARPT
WST	WESTERLY, RI
PBI	WEST PALM BEACH, FL
WYS	WEST YELLOWSTONE, MT
HLG	WHEELING, WV
HPN	WHITE PLAINS, NY
ICT	WICHITA, KS
SPS	WICHITA FALLS, TX
AVP	WILKES-BARRE/SCRANTON, PA
IPT	WILLIAMSPORT, PA
ILG	WILMINGTON, DE
ILM	WILMINGTON, NC
YQG	WINDSOR, ONT., CANADA
YWG	WINNIPEG, MAN., CANADA
INW	WINSLOW, AZ
INT	WINSTON SALEM, NC
ISW	WISCONSIN RAPIDS, WI
ORH	WORCESTER, MA

Y

YKM	YAKIMA, WA
YKN	YANKTON, SD
OYS	YOSEMITE NATIONAL PARK, CA
YNG	YOUNGSTOWN, OH
YUM	YUMA, AZ

Z

ZAG	ZAGREB, YUGOSLAVIA
ZIH	ZIHUATANEJO, MEXICO
ZRH	ZURICH, SWITZERLAND

APPENDIX E
AIR MILES BETWEEN CITIES AROUND THE WORLD

SOURCE: DEFENSE MAPPING AGENCY AEROSPACE CENTER (STATUTE MILES)
POINT TO POINT MEASUREMENTS ARE USUALLY FROM CITY HALL

	Bangkok	Berlin	Cairo	Cape-town	Caracas	Chicago	Hong Kong	Hono-lulu	Lima	London
Bangkok	—	5,352	4,523	6,300	10,555	8,570	1,077	6,609	1,244	5,944
Berlin	5,352	—	1,797	5,961	5,238	4,414	5,443	7,320	6,896	583
Cairo	4,523	1,797	—	4,480	6,342	6,141	5,066	8,848	7,726	2,185
Capetown	6,300	5,961	4,480	—	6,366	8,491	7,376	11,535	6,072	5,989
Caracas	10,555	5,238	6,342	6,366	—	2,495	10,165	6,021	1,707	4,655
Chicago	8,570	4,414	6,141	8,491	2,495	—	7,797	4,256	3,775	3,958
Hong Kong	1,077	5,443	5,066	7,376	10,165	7,797	—	5,556	11,418	5,990
Honolulu	6,609	7,320	8,848	11,535	6,021	4,256	5,556	—	5,947	7,240
London	5,944	583	2,185	5,989	4,655	3,958	5,990	7,240	6,316	—
Madrid	6,337	1,165	2,087	5,308	4,346	4,189	6,558	7,872	5,907	785
Melbourne	4,568	9,918	8,675	6,425	9,717	9,673	4,595	5,505	8,059	10,500
Mexico City	9,793	6,056	7,700	8,519	2,234	1,690	8,788	3,789	2,639	5,558
Montreal	8,338	3,740	5,427	7,922	2,438	745	7,736	4,918	3,970	3,254
Moscow	4,389	1,006	1,803	6,279	6,177	4,987	4,437	7,047	7,862	1,564

	Bangkok	Berlin	Cairo	Cape-town	Caracas	Chicago	Hong Kong	Hono-lulu	Lima	London
New Delhi	1,813	3,598	2,758	5,769	8,833	7,486	2,339	7,412	10,432	4,181
New York	8,669	3,979	5,619	7,803	2,120	714	8,060	4,969	3,639	3,469
Paris	5,877	548	1,998	5,786	4,732	4,143	5,990	7,449	6,370	214
Peking	2,046	4,584	4,698	8,044	8,950	6,604	1,217	5,077	10,349	5,074
Rio de Janeiro	9,994	6,209	6,143	3,781	2,804	5,282	11,009	8,288	2,342	5,750
Rome	5,494	737	1,326	5,231	5,195	4,824	5,774	8,040	6,750	895
San Francisco	7,931	5,672	7,466	10,248	3,902	1,859	6,905	2,398	4,518	5,367
Singapore	883	6,164	5,137	6,008	11,402	9,372	1,605	6,726	11,689	6,747
Stockholm	5,089	528	2,096	6,423	5,471	4,331	5,063	6,875	7,166	942
Tokyo	2,865	5,557	5,958	9,154	8,808	6,314	1,791	3,859	9,631	5,959
Warsaw	5,033	322	1,619	5,935	5,559	4,679	5,147	7,366	7,215	905
Washington, D.C.	8,807	4,181	5,822	7,895	2,047	596	8,155	4,838	3,509	3,674

	Madrid	Mel-bourne	Mexico City	Mon-treal	Mos-cow	Nai-robi	New Delhi	New York	Paris	Peking
Bangkok	6,337	4,568	9,793	8,338	4,389	4,483	1,813	8,669	5,877	2,046
Berlin	1,165	9,918	6,056	3,740	1,006	3,949	3,598	3,979	548	4,584
Cairo	2,087	8,675	7,700	5,427	1,803	2,186	2,758	5,619	1,998	4,698
Capetown	5,308	6,425	8,519	7,922	6,279	2,542	5,769	7,803	5,786	8,044
Caracas	4,346	9,717	2,234	2,438	6,177	7,178	8,833	2,120	4,732	8,950
Chicago	4,189	9,673	1,690	745	4,987	8,011	7,486	714	4,143	6,604
Hong Kong	6,558	4,595	8,788	7,736	4,437	5,449	2,339	8,060	5,990	1,217
Honolulu	7,872	5,505	3,789	4,918	7,047	10,741	7,412	4,969	7,449	5,077
London	785	10,500	5,558	3,254	1,564	4,231	4,181	3,469	214	5,074
Madrid	—	10,758	5,643	3,448	2,147	3,841	4,530	3,593	655	5,745
Melbourne	10,758	—	8,426	10,395	8,950	7,153	6,329	10,359	10,430	5,643
Mexico City	5,643	8,426	—	2,317	6,676	9,219	9,120	2,090	5,725	7,753
Montreal	3,448	10,395	2,317	—	4,401	7,267	7,012	331	3,432	6,519

	Madrid	Melbourne	Mexico City	Montreal	Moscow	Nairobi	New Delhi	New York	Paris	Peking
Moscow	2,147	8,950	6,676	4,401	—	3,930	2,698	4,683	1,554	3,607
New Delhi	4,530	6,329	9,120	7,012	2,698	3,374	—	7,318	4,102	2,353
New York	3,593	10,359	2,090	331	4,683	7,364	7,318	—	3,636	6,844
Paris	655	10,430	5,725	3,432	1,554	4,022	4,102	3,636	—	5,120
Peking	5,745	5,643	7,753	6,519	3,607	5,727	2,353	6,844	5,120	—
Rio de Janeiro	5,045	8,226	4,764	5,078	7,170	5,560	8,753	4,801	5,684	10,768
Rome	851	9,929	6,377	4,104	1,483	3,339	3,684	4,293	690	5,063
San Francisco	5,803	7,856	1,887	2,543	5,885	9,597	7,691	2,572	5,577	5,918
Singapore	7,080	3,759	10,327	9,203	5,228	4,638	2,571	9,534	6,673	2,771
Stockholm	1,653	9,630	6,012	3,714	716	4,281	3,414	3,986	1,003	4,133
Tokyo	6,706	5,062	7,035	6,471	4,660	6,999	3,638	6,757	6,053	1,307
Warsaw	1,427	9,598	6,337	4,022	721	3,801	3,277	4,270	852	4,325
Washington, D.C.	3,792	10,180	1,885	489	4,876	7,551	7,500	205	3,840	6,942

	Rio de Janeiro	Rome	San Francisco	Singapore	Stockholm	Teheran	Tokyo	Vienna	Warsaw	Wash., D.C.
Bangkok	9,994	5,494	7,931	883	5,089	3,391	2,865	5,252	5,033	8,807
Berlin	6,209	737	5,672	6,164	528	2,185	5,557	326	322	4,181
Cairo	6,143	1,326	7,466	5,137	2,096	1,234	5,958	1,481	1,619	5,822
Capetown	3,781	5,231	10,248	6,008	6,423	5,241	9,154	5,656	5,935	7,895
Caracas	2,804	5,195	3,902	11,402	5,471	7,320	8,808	5,372	5,559	2,047
Chicago	5,282	4,824	1,859	9,372	4,331	6,502	6,314	4,698	4,679	596
Hong Kong	11,009	5,774	6,905	1,605	5,063	3,843	1,791	5,431	5,147	8,155
Honolulu	8,288	8,040	2,398	6,726	6,875	8,070	3,859	7,632	7,366	4,838
London	5,750	895	5,367	6,747	942	2,743	5,959	771	905	3,674
Madrid	5,045	851	5,803	7,080	1,653	2,978	6,706	1,128	1,427	3,792
Melbourne	8,226	9,929	7,856	3,759	9,630	7,826	5,062	9,790	9,598	10,180
Mexico City	4,764	6,377	1,887	10,327	6,012	8,184	7,035	6,320	6,337	1,885

	Rio de Janiero	Rome	San Francisco	Singapore	Stockholm	Teheran	Tokyo	Vienna	Warsaw	Wash., D.C.
Montreal	5,078	4,104	2,543	9,203	3,714	5,880	6,471	4,009	4,022	489
Moscow	7,170	1,483	5,885	5,228	716	1,532	4,660	1,043	721	4,876
New Delhi	8,753	3,684	7,691	2,571	3,414	1,583	3,638	3,465	3,277	7,500
New York	4,801	4,293	2,572	9,534	3,986	6,141	6,757	4,234	4,270	205
Paris	5,684	690	5,577	6,673	1,003	2,625	6,053	645	852	3,840
Peking	10,768	5,063	5,918	2,771	4,133	3,490	1,307	4,648	4,325	6,942
Rio de Janeiro	—	5,707	6,613	9,785	6,683	7,374	11,532	6,127	6,455	4,779
Rome	5,707	—	6,259	6,229	1,245	2,127	6,142	477	820	4,497
San Francisco	6,613	6,259	—	8,448	5,399	7,362	5,150	5,994	5,854	2,441
Singapore	9,785	6,229	8,448	—	5,936	4,103	3,300	6,035	5,843	9,662
Stockholm	6,683	1,245	5,399	5,936	—	2,173	5,053	780	494	4,183
Tokyo	11,532	6,142	5,150	3,300	5,053	4,775	—	5,689	5,347	6,791
Warsaw	6,455	820	5,854	5,843	494	1,879	5,689	347	—	4,472
Washington, D.C.	4,779	4,497	2,441	9,662	4,183	6,341	6,791	4,438	4,472	—

APPENDIX F
AIRCRAFT PERFORMANCE STATISTICS

This list of the various types of passenger jet aircraft in use by American and foreign companies explains the differences in speed, weight, passenger load and plane size between each craft.

The code listed on the left margin will aid you when reading timetables. At last you will be able to tell what kind of aircraft you are scheduled to fly on.

AIRCRAFT PERFORMANCE STATISTICS

Code	Type of Aircraft	No. of Engines	Total Horse-power	Wing Span ft.	Wing Span in.	Plane Length ft.	Plane Length in.	Gross Weight (lbs.)	Passenger Capacity	Cruising Speed (m.p.h.)	Range Miles
AB3	Airbus Industrie A300B	2	102,000	147	1	175	11	313,060	201/345	576	2,100
B11	Bac 111 (all series)	2	20,820	88	6	93	6	78,500	74/79	550	1,430
707	Boeing 707 passenger jet (all series)	4	52,000	130	10	145	1	248,000	100/159	585	3,300
70M	Boeing 707 (mixed passenger/freighter)	4	76,000	145	9	152	11	333,600	/147	600	5,200
B72	Boeing 720	4	348,000	130	10	136	9	225,000	92/144	600	3,300
727	Boeing 727 passenger jet (all series)	3	43,500	108	0	133	2	169,000	94	605	2,600
72S	Boeing 727-200	3	48,000	108	0	153	2	197,000	134	605	1,600

Code	Type of Aircraft	No. of Engines	Total Horse-power	Wing Span ft.	in.	Plane Length ft.	in.	Gross Weight (lbs.)	Passenger Capacity	Cruising Speed (m.p.h.)	Range Miles
737	Boeing 737 passenger jet (all series)	2	28,000	93	0	94	0	97,800	101	575	1,840
73S	Boeing 737-200	2	32,000	93	0	100	0	117,000	115	573	2,000
73M	Boeing 737-200 (mixed passenger/freighter)	2	32,000	93	0	100	0	117,000	115	573	1,800
747	Boeing 747 passenger jet (all series except SP)	4	194,280	195	8	231	4	710,000	395	625	5,500
74L	Boeing 747 SP	4	192,000	195	8	184	9	660,000	300	650	8,200
CRV	Caravelle (all series)	2	29,000	112	6	118	10	127,870	128/140	512	2,150
CVR	Convair (all series prop/turboprop)	2	7,500	105	4	79	2	54,600	56	350	1,100
CV8	Convair 880	4	44,800	120	0	129	4	193,000	90/104	615	2,994
LOE	Lockheed Electra Turboprop	4	15,000	99	0	104	6½	116,000	66/104	405	2,750
L10	Lockheed L1011 (all series)	3	126,000	155	4	177	8	466,000	256/400	600	4,560
DC8	McDonnell Douglas DC8 (all series)	4	54,000	142	4	150	8	265,000	120/168	550	3,500
D8S	McDonnell Douglas DC-8 (all 60 series)	4	72,000	142	4	187	5	325,000	180/259	600	3,700
D8M	McDonnell Douglas DC-8 (mixed passenger/freighter)	4	72,000	142	4	187	5	325,000	180/259	600	3,700
DC9	McDonnell Douglas DC9-10 and 20 series	2	28,000	89	5	104	5	90,700	72/90	560	2,000
D9S	McDonnell Douglas DC9-30 and 40 series	2	31,000	93	4	125	7	114,000	94/115	560	1,674
D95	McDonnell Douglas DC9-50	2	31,000	93	4	133	7	121,000	139	560	2,025
D10	McDonnell Douglas DC10 (all series)	3	123,000/ 162,000	155 to 165	4/ 4	181	5	455,000/ 572,000	255/380	600	4,400/ 7,400
SSC	Supersonic Concorde	4	152,200	83	10	203	9	400,000	108/123	1,400	3,800
VCX	Vickers VC10 (all series)	4	84,000	146	2	158	8	312,000	135/151	555	5,650
VCP	Vickers Vanguard (passenger)	4	22,100	118	0	122	10½	146,500	97/139	405	2,910

GLOSSARY OF TERMS

Cancellation insurance—Low-cost insurance available to the consumer to protect him from unexpected expenses incurred when a charter or a tour company cancels his flight, or low-cost insurance available to the consumer to protect him from penalties charged if for any reason he is not able to make a charter flight that has been prepaid.

Charter—A class of air transportation that now includes both group and individual travelers who purchase round-trip tickets for specific dates at discount prices.

Customs—The regulatory agency of any country that controls the movement of people and goods across national borders.

Declaration—The statement travelers make to the customs service about the amount of foreign goods they are bringing into the country. Also see oral declaration, written declaration.

Excursion—A class of air fare that allows a traveler to purchase a round-trip ticket for less than the regular coach fare if he travels within a minimum and maximum number of days.

Feeder Lines—Any of the airlines in the U.S. that serve the smaller towns and cities of the country and connect these regional centers to the large metropolitan airports.

Free Baggage Allowance—The amount of luggage any one passenger is permitted to have on a flight without charge.

Group Fare—A broad category of airline fares that require that the purchaser travel as a member of a group for at least the duration of the flight. Group Fares are explained in detail in chapter five.

GIT—Group Inclusive Travel is an air fare plan that combines group air travel with mandatory land arrangements.

TGC—Travel Group Charter is an air fare-only plan that offers large savings and many potential snags.

Affinity Group—an air fare that is available to any cohesive group or club that travels together throughout the entire trip.

Immigration—The government service that supervises the entrance of citizens and aliens into a country. When traveling, you will go through immigration before you pick up your baggage or go through customs.

Individual Fares—These fares, although they may be based on a minimum number of passengers signing up for the flight, do not require that you concern yourself with the group.

ITX—Individual Tour Basing Fares are prepaid land and air plans that allow individual travel.

OTC—One Stop Tour Charters offer passengers more than one stop. The only requirement is that you begin and end your trip at the same airport. The drawback? Charter may be canceled at last minute if not enough people sign up. You must buy land arrangements with this plan.

ABC—Advanced Booking Charter must be bought at least 30–45 days in advance. Savings are 50 percent over coach. No land purchase necessary.

ITC—Inclusive Tour Charters requires that you prepay for air and land. You must stop in three cities. No advanced purchase required.

Intra-European Airlines—All European national airlines and smaller regional airlines offer fare breaks on travel within Europe only. These fares must be given to you by a travel agent upon request. Discounts are sometimes greater because of currency exchanges, if purchased while abroad.

Jet Lag—This popular term for the feeling of fatigue that overcomes long-distance travelers is actually a description of the feelings that happen when your circadian rhythm is disturbed.

Landing Forms—These forms, handed out to all passengers on international flights, are for the information of the customs and immigration officials at your destination. The forms include information about your itinerary and your possessions.

Landing Gear—Not a gear at all really, this is the entire wheel mechanism that is lowered during descent (and raised after takeoff), making strange noises that are often frightening to the unaware.

Land Purchase Requirements—This term, associated with charter and tour air plans, means that a traveler must prepay for hotel, sight-seeing, or cultural events in order to take advantage of the low airfare offered by the charter tour.

Open-Jaw—This ridiculous term means that the air fare plan you have permits you to return home from a third point. For example, if you left New York and landed in Frankfurt, you may return home from Paris instead of Frankfurt for the same price. This term is applied to discount fares only.

Oral Declaration—If you do not have any duty-due goods to declare at customs, you may state that fact. Purchases worth less than a total of $300 are included in an oral declaration.

Overbooking—A practice by the airlines that jeopardizes all reserved seats by selling more tickets than there are seats on a plane. The reasons for this are complex and the results can spell disaster.

Passport—The document issued by a country to identify the bearer as a citizen.

Reconfirmation—All international travelers must reconfirm their ticket reservations by calling the airlines at least 72 hours before the departure of their flight. Failure to do so can result in cancellation of the reservation.

Standby—An old practice revived now for international passengers, it offers very low prices for patient passengers who buy seats on an "availability" basis—if they are available you get a seat—if they are not, you wait until a seat is available.

Travel Agent—A liaison between you and the airline, hotel or tour company. Agents provide a free booking service to travelers and can often provide complete information on all aspects of a trip.

Trunk Lines—A term that designates the major airlines in the U.S. These companies serve the large metropolitan airports across the country. American and TWA are examples of such lines.

Turbulence—An aeronautical term that describes any air disturbance that causes the aircraft to be buffeted around. There is both clear and bad weather turbulence. It is rarely dangerous.

Visa—A form authorizing the entrance of an alien into any country for a limited period of time; a visa is usually a stamp in your passport.

Weekend Fares—There are two conditions in which weekend travel costs either more or less than midweek travel. International flights sometimes charge travelers an additional $15 fee for eastbound travel on Fridays or Saturdays and westbound travel on Saturdays or Sundays. Domestic flights offer weekend excursion fares for reduced rates.

Written Declaration—If you are bringing more than $300 worth of foreign purchases into this country, you must fill out a form stating the nature and price of all your purchases. Duty is charged on items that have to be declared.